W9-AFX-363

SCRIPTURES TO LIVE BY
PEARLS

Publisher's Cataloging in Publication
(prepared by Quality Books Inc.)

Pearls: scriptures to live by / compiled by Brian Campbell.
p. cm.
Includes index.
Pre-assigned LCCN: 93-086763
ISBN 0-9636730-0-9

1. Bible-Quotations. 2. Meditations. 3. Mental Health—
Religious Aspects. I. Campbell, Brian M.

BS416.P43 1993   220'.088'082
                                  QBI93-21814

New Horizons Press
PO Box 951555
Lake Mary, FL 32795-1555

Ordering Information:
Tel: 1-800-99-PEARLS

New! Ask about PEARLS on tape.

ISBN 0-9636730-0-9

Printed in the United States of America

To Claire
...my dearest love
...my earthly pearl

ACKNOWLEDGMENTS

To my wife, Claire, who was the wind beneath my wings and the silent strength that supported this endeavor to its completion.

To my children, Amy, Shawn, and Colin, whom I love more than the sun and the moon and the stars. I earnestly pray that these scriptures will help bring you to the feet of Jesus so that together we might dwell in the house of the Lord forever.

To the memory of my father, Matthew Campbell, and to my mother, Lura, who trained me and raised me to walk in the way of the Lord. I am eternally grateful for your guidance and instruction.

To Dr. Thomas A. Walsh, for his continual support and encouragement in completing this book.

To Pauline Hillestad, who helped me squeeze out enough time in my schedule to finish this project and who was my sounding board on many different aspects of the book. To Norm Hillestad who provided well-needed biblical scholarship and resources, and to Stephanie Hillestad who helped me proofread the final version of the book.

And to Rob Kerby of Publications Technologies Services.

CONTENTS

INTRODUCTION

The Bible is overflowing with pearls of wisdom and knowledge! Whatever your problem, concern, or topic of interest may be, God has provided valuable guidance and instruction in the inspired writings contained in His Word.

This collection of scriptures grew out of my work as a Christian therapist. The book is overflowing with quotations that will help restore mental health and provide needed guidance and comfort in times of crisis.

However, it is my firm belief that God's Word should not be consulted solely during difficult situations or under conditions of emotional turmoil. I earnestly pray that you will find a wide range of additional uses for this book.

For parents, I invite you to utilize these scriptures for purposes of training and instruction. Feed your children on God's Word on a regular basis. The biblical truths that God has revealed will help counteract the secular "lies" that are being taught by modern society.

For the Christian adult, I recommend that you use this book as part of your daily Bible study and prayer. Have it available, along with the Bible, when you are witnessing to others. Give a copy to nonbelievers. Use it during discussion groups, and as a tool for memorizing scriptures and hiding the Word of God in your heart.

The production of this book has been life-changing for me. At times, I have been totally overwhelmed by the awesome Word of God. As I collected the scriptures under different topical headings, the incredible consistency and harmony of the Bible emerged in new and exciting ways for me.

The Word of God is powerful and persuasive. Although it is often convenient for human beings to ignore or overlook certain passages, it is exceedingly difficult to ignore the force of ten to twenty scriptures that all harken to the same theme or topic.

As you explore this book, I invite you to make it a habit of reading all of the scriptures contained under a particular topic. For the most part, you will find that the quotations "flow together" and combine to provide a clear and consistent lesson on a particular subject.

Next, after reading all of the scriptures on a particular topic, mark any passages that are of special interest to you and then use the cross-reference key provided at the top of the page to locate related topics of interest.

Finally, return to the Bible and look up any scriptures you have marked and study them in their original context to obtain additional meaning and understanding.

I do not profess to be a Bible scholar, and I have had to rely on God's inspiration to help me collect these scriptures and arrange them under meaningful topics. If I have made mistakes in the placement of particular scriptures, or if I have left out important quotations, I invite my brothers and sisters in Christ to provide me with necessary guidance and direction so that I may make the necessary corrections in any subsequent editions of this book.

Yours in Christ,
Brian Campbell, Ph.D.

ABORTION

For you created my inmost
being; you knit me together
in my mother's womb.
(Psalm 139:13)

Your hands made me and
formed me.
(Psalm 119:3)

Before I formed you in the womb I knew you, before you
were born I set you apart.
(Jeremiah 1:5)

I praise you because I am fearfully and wonderfully
made; your works are wonderful, I know that full well.
(Psalm 139:14)

My frame was not hidden from you when I was made in
the secret place. When I was woven together in the
depths of the earth, your eyes saw my unformed body.
(Psalm 139:15-16)

This is what the LORD says — he who made you, who
formed you in the womb.
(Isaiah 44:2)

When Elizabeth heard Mary's greeting, the baby leaped
in her womb, and Elizabeth was filled with the Holy
Spirit.
(Luke 1:41)

From birth I was cast upon you; from my mother's womb
you have been my God.
(Psalm 22:10)

Yet you brought me out of the womb; you made me trust
in you even at my mother's breast.
(Psalm 22:19)

From birth I have relied on you; you brought me forth
from my mother's womb. I will ever praise you.
(Psalm 71:6)

All the days ordained for me were written in your book
before one of them came to be.
(Psalm 139:16)

For we must all appear before the judgment seat of
Christ, that each one may receive what is due him for the
things done while in the body, whether good or bad.
(2 Corinthians 5:10)

I have set before you life and death, blessings and curses.
Now choose life, so that you and your children may live
and that you may love the LORD your God, listen to his
voice, and hold fast to him.
(Deuteronomy 30:19-20)

If we confess our sins, he is faithful and just and will
forgive us our sins and purify us from all
unrighteousness.
(1 John 1:9)

ACTION

See also:
Disobedience
Fruitful
Giving
Obedience
Righteous
Self-Sacrifice
Witness

Dear children, let us not love with words or tongue but with actions and in truth.
(1 John 3:18)

Do not merely listen to the word, and so deceive yourselves. Do what it says.
(James 1:22)

For it is not those who hear the law who are righteous in God's sight, but it is those who obey the law who will be declared righteous.
(Romans 2:13)

Live such good lives among the pagans that, though they accuse you of doing wrong, they may see your good deeds and glorify God on the day he visits us.
(1 Peter 2:12)

Who is wise and understanding among you? Let him show it by his good life, by deeds done in the humility that comes from wisdom.
(James 3:13)

Do not withhold good from those who deserve it, when it is in your power to act. Do not say to your neighbor, "Come back later; I'll give it tomorrow" — when you now have it with you.
(Proverbs 3:27-28)

What good is it, my brothers, if a man claims to have faith but has no deeds? Can such faith save him? Suppose a brother or sister is without clothes and daily food.

If one of you says to him, "Go, I wish you well; keep warm and well fed," but does nothing about his physical needs, what good is it? In the same way, faith by itself, if it is not accompanied by action, is dead.
(James 2:14-17)

Show me your faith without deeds, and I will show you my faith by what I do.
(James 2:18)

They claim to know God, but by their actions they deny him.
(Titus 1:16)

You foolish man, do you want evidence that faith without deeds is useless? Was not our ancestor Abraham considered righteous for what he did when he offered his son Isaac on the altar? You see that his faith and his actions were working together, and his faith was made complete by what he did.
(James 2:20-22)

A person is justified by what he does and not by faith alone.
(James 2:24)

As the body without the spirit is dead, so faith without deeds is dead.
(James 2:26)

Now that you know these things, you will be blessed if you do them.
(John 13:17)

I tell you the truth, anyone who has faith in me will do what I have been doing. He will do even greater things than these, because I am going to the Father.
(John 14:12)

I will show you what he is like who comes to me and hears my words and puts them into practice. He is like a man building a house, who dug down deep and laid the foundation on rock. When a flood came, the torrent struck that house but could not shake it, because it was well built.
(Luke 6:47-48)

But the one who hears my words and does not put them into practice is like a man who built a house on the ground without a foundation. The moment the torrent struck that house, it collapsed and its destruction was complete.
(Luke 6:49)

My mother and brothers are those who hear God's word and put it into practice.
(Luke 8:21)

Whatever you have learned or received or heard from me, or seen in me — put into practice. And the God of peace will be with you.
(Philippians 4:9)

ADOLESCENT GUIDANCE

See also:
Adolescent Rebellion
Discipline
Disobedience
Friendship
Obedience
Parenting
Ten Commandments
Wisdom

Don't let anyone look down on you because you are young, but set an example for the believers in speech, in life, in love, in faith and in purity.
(1 Timothy 4:12)

Be happy, young man, while you are young, and let your heart give you joy in the days of your youth. Follow the ways of your heart and whatever your eyes see, but know that for all these things God will bring you to judgment.
(Ecclesiastes 11:9)

Hold on to instruction, do not let it go; guard it well, for it is your life.
(Proverbs 4:13)

My son, preserve sound judgment and discernment, do not let them out of your sight; they will be life for you, an ornament to grace your neck. Then you will go on your way in safety, and your foot will not stumble; when you lie down, you will not be afraid; when you lie down, your sleep will be sweet.
(Proverbs 3:21-24)

My son, keep your father's commands and do not forsake your mother's teaching. Bind them upon your heart forever; fasten them around your neck. When you walk, they will guide you; when you sleep, they will watch over you; when you awake, they will speak to you.
(Proverbs 6:20-22)

Listen to advice and accept instruction, and in the end you will be wise.
(Proverbs 19:20)

My son, if your heart is wise, then my heart will be glad; my inmost being will rejoice when your lips speak what is right.
(Proverbs 23:15-16)

Listen, my son, and be wise, and keep your heart on the right path.
(Proverbs 23:19)

My son, give me your heart and let your eyes keep to my ways.
(Proverbs 23:26)

Be wise, my son, and bring joy to my heart.
(Proverbs 27:11)

He who walks with the wise grows wise, but a companion of fools suffers harm.
(Proverbs 13:20)

Do not be misled: "Bad company corrupts good character."
(1 Corinthians 15:33)

My son, if sinners entice you, do not give in to them.
(Proverbs 1:10)

Honor your father and mother ... so that it may go well with you and that you may enjoy long life on the earth.
(Ephesians 6:2)

Children, obey your parents in everything, for this pleases the Lord.
(Colossians 3:20)

May your father and mother be glad; may she who gave
you birth rejoice!
(Proverbs 23:25)

Since my youth, O God, you have taught me, and to this
day I declare your marvelous deeds.
(Psalm 71:17)

How can a young man keep his way pure? By living
according to your word.
(Psalm 119:9)

ADOLESCENT REBELLION

See also:
Adolescent Guidance
Discipline
Disobedience
Friendship
Obedience
Parenting
Ten Commandments
Wisdom

Fear the LORD and the king, my son, and do not join with the rebellious.
(Proverbs 24:21)

Do not set foot on the path of the wicked or walk in the way of evil men.
(Proverbs 4:14)

The eye that mocks a father, that scorns obedience to a mother, will be pecked out by the ravens of the valley, will be eaten by the vultures.
(Proverbs 30:17)

A wise son brings joy to his father, but a foolish son grief to his mother.
(Proverbs 10:1)

A wise son heeds his father's instruction, but a mocker does not listen to rebuke.
(Proverbs 13:1)

He who scorns instruction will pay for it, but he who respects a command is rewarded.
(Proverbs 13:13)

Children, obey your parents in the Lord, for this is right.
(Ephesians 6:1)

Listen, my son, to your father's instruction and do not forsake your mother's teaching.
(Proverbs 1:8)

Listen to your father, who gave you life, and do not despise your mother when she is old.
(Proverbs 23:22)

He who ignores discipline despises himself, but whoever heeds correction gains understanding.
(Proverbs 15:32)

A fool spurns his father's discipline, but whoever heeds correction shows prudence.
(Proverbs 15:5)

My son, do not despise the LORD's discipline and do not resent his rebuke, because the LORD disciplines those he loves, as a father, the son he delights in.
(Proverbs 3:11-12)

A foolish son brings grief to his father and bitterness to the one who bore him.
(Proverbs 17:25)

Cursed is the man who dishonors his father or his mother.
(Deuteronomy 27:16)

There are those who curse their fathers and do not bless their mothers.
(Proverbs 30:11)

A wise son brings joy to his father, but a foolish man despises his mother.
(Proverbs 15:20)

To have a fool for a son brings grief; there is no joy for the father of a fool.
(Proverbs 17:21)

He who robs his father and drives out his mother is a son who brings shame and disgrace.
(Proverbs 19:26)

Even a child is known by his actions, by whether his conduct is pure and right.
(Proverbs 20:11)

At the end of your life you will groan, when your flesh and body are spent. You will say, "How I hated discipline! How my heart spurned correction! I would not obey my teachers or listen to my instructors. I have come to the brink of utter ruin in the midst of the whole assembly."
(Proverbs 5:11-14)

ADULTERY

See also:
Divorce
Lust
Marriage
Promiscuity
Prostitution
Sex, Normal
Temptation
Ten Commandments

You shall not commit adultery.
(Deuteronomy 5:18)

Do not have sexual relations
with your neighbor's wife and
defile yourself with her.
(Leviticus 18:20)

A man who commits adultery lacks judgement; whoever
does so destroys himself.
(Proverbs 6:32)

Why be captivated, my son, by an adulteress? Why
embrace the bosom of another man's wife? For a man's
ways are in full view of the LORD, and he examines all his
paths. The evil deeds of a wicked man ensnare him; the
cords of his sin hold him fast.
(Proverbs 5:20-22)

Can a man scoop fire into his lap without his clothes
being burned? Can a man walk on hot coals without his
feet being scorched? So is he who sleeps with another
man's wife; no one who touches her will go unpunished.
(Proverbs 6:27-29)

The eye of the adulterer watches for dusk; he thinks, "No
eye will see me," and he keeps his face concealed.
(Job 24:15)

With eyes full of adultery, they never stop sinning; they
seduce the unstable; they are experts in greed — an
accursed brood!
(2 Peter 2:14)

I supplied all their needs, yet they committed adultery and thronged to the houses of prostitutes.
(Jeremiah 5:7)

The lips of an adulteress drip honey, and her speech is smoother than oil; but in the end she is bitter gall, sharp as a double-edged sword.
(Proverbs 5:3)

The mouth of an adulteress is a deep pit; he who is under the LORD's wrath will fall into it.
(Proverbs 22:14)

This is the way of an adulteress: She eats and wipes her mouth and says, "I've done nothing wrong."
(Proverbs 30:20)

Her feet go down to death; her steps lead straight to the grave.
(Proverbs 5:5)

Keep to a path far from her, do not go near the door of her house, lest you give your best strength to others and your years to one who is cruel, lest strangers feast on your wealth and your toil enrich another man's house.
(Proverbs 5:8-10)

For her house leads down to death and her paths to the spirits of the dead. None who go to her return or attain the paths of life.
(Proverbs 2:18-19)

Say to wisdom, "You are my sister," and call understanding your kinsman; they will keep you from the adulteress, from the wayward wife with her seductive words.
(Proverbs 7:4-5)

If we deliberately keep on sinning after we have received
the knowledge of the truth, no sacrifice for sins is left, but
only a fearful expectation of judgment and of raging fire
that will consume the enemies of God.
(Hebrews 10:26-27)

ALCOHOLISM

See also:
Anxiety/Worry
Backsliding
Dissatisfaction
Drug Abuse
Guilt/Shame
Hopeless
Repent
Self-Esteem, Low
Temptation
Weakness

Who has woe? Who has sorrow?
Who has strife? Who has complaints?
Who has needless bruises? Who has
bloodshot eyes? Those who linger
over wine, who go to sample bowls
of mixed wine.
(Proverbs 23:29-30)

Do not gaze at wine when it is red, when it sparkles in the
cup, when it goes down smoothly! In the end it bites like a
snake and poisons like a viper.
(Proverbs 23:31-32)

Do not get drunk on wine, which leads to debauchery.
Instead, be filled with the Holy Spirit.
(Ephesians 5:18)

Woe to those who rise early in the morning to run after
their drinks, who stay up late at night till they are inflamed with wine.
(Isaiah 5:11)

Woe to those who are heroes at drinking wine and
champions at mixing drinks.
(Isaiah 5:22)

Woe to him who gives drink to his neighbors, pouring it
from the wineskin till they are drunk, so that he can gaze on their
naked bodies. You will be filled with shame instead of glory.
(Habakkuk 2:15-16)

Wine is a mocker and beer a brawler; whoever is led
astray by them is not wise.
(Proverbs 20:1)

He who loves pleasure will become poor; whoever loves wine and oil will never be rich.
(Proverbs 21:17)

In the streets they cry out for wine; all joy turns to gloom, all gaiety is banished from the earth.
(Isaiah 24:11)

Do not join those who drink too much wine or gorge themselves on meat, for drunkards and gluttons become poor, and drowsiness clothes them in rags.
(Proverbs 23:20-21)

Your eyes will see strange sights and your mind imagine confusing things.
(Proverbs 23:33)

You will be like one sleeping on the high seas, lying on top of the rigging.
(Proverbs 23:34)

"They hit me," you will say, "but I'm not hurt! They beat me, but I don't feel it! When will I wake up so I can find another drink?"
(Proverbs 23:35)

I do not understand what I do. For what I want to do I do not do, but what I hate I do.
(Romans 7:15)

For in my inner being I delight in God's law; but I see another law at work in the members of my body, waging war against the law of my mind and making me a prisoner of the law of sin at work within my members.
(Romans 7:22-23)

ANGER

See also:
Forgive
Hatred
Impatient
Judgmental
Love, For Others
Peace
Vengeance

Do not be quickly provoked in your spirit, for anger resides in the lap of fools.
(Ecclesiastes 7:9)

Everyone should be quick to listen, slow to speak and slow to become angry, for man's anger does not bring about the righteous life that God desires.
(James 1:19-20)

Refrain from anger and turn from wrath.
(Psalm 37:8)

A fool gives full vent to his anger, but a wise man keeps himself under control.
(Proverbs 29:11)

In your anger do not sin.
(Psalm 4:4)

Do not let the sun go down while you are still angry and do not give the devil a foothold.
(Ephesians 4:26-27)

I want men everywhere to lift up holy hands in prayer, without anger or disputing.
(1 Timothy 2:8)

Make every effort to live in peace with all men.
(Hebrews 12:14)

A quick-tempered man does foolish things.
(Proverbs 14:17)

A hot-tempered man stirs up dissension, but a patient man calms a quarrel.
(Proverbs 15:18)

For as churning the milk produces butter, and as twisting the nose produces blood, so stirring up anger produces strife.
(Proverbs 30:33)

A violent man entices his neighbor and leads him down a path that is not good.
(Proverbs 16:29)

Do not make friends with a hot-tempered man, do not associate with one easily angered, or you may learn his ways and get yourself ensnared.
(Proverbs 22:24-25)

An angry man stirs up dissension, and a hot-tempered one commits many sins.
(Proverbs 29:22)

Wise men turn away anger.
(Proverbs 29:8)

A hot-tempered man must pay the penalty; if you rescue him, you will have to do it again.
(Proverbs 19:19)

But I tell you that anyone who is angry with his brother will be subject to judgement. Again, anyone who says to his brother "Raca," is answerable to the Sanhedrin. But anyone who says, "You fool!" will be in danger of the fire of hell.
(Matthew 5:22)

ANTICHRIST

See also:
Devil
End Times
Evil, Resisting
Occult
Temptation

Dear children, this is the last hour;
and as you have heard that the antichrist is coming, even now many
antichrists have come.
(1 John 2:18)

Who is the liar? It is the man who denies that Jesus is the
Christ. Such a man is the antichrist — he denies the
Father and the Son.
(1 John 2:22)

Dear friends, do not believe every spirit, but test the
spirits to see whether they are from God, because many
false prophets have gone out into the world.
(1 John 4:1)

This is how you can recognize the Spirit of God: Every spirit
that acknowledges that Jesus Christ has come in the flesh is
from God, but every spirit that does not acknowledge Jesus
is not from God. This is the spirit of the antichrist, which you
have heard is coming and even now is already in the world.
(1 John 4:2-3)

Many deceivers, who do not acknowledge Jesus Christ as
coming in the flesh, have gone out into the world. Any
such person is the deceiver and the antichrist.
(2 John 1:7)

*For many will come in my name, claiming, "I am the Christ,"
and will deceive many.*
(Matthew 24:5)

And many false prophets will appear and deceive many people.
(Matthew 24:11)

Watch out that you do not lose what you have worked for, but that you may be rewarded fully.
(2 John 1:8)

Watch out for false prophets. They come to you in sheep's clothing, but inwardly they are ferocious wolves. By their fruit you will recognize them.
(Matthew 7:15-16)

Watch out that no one deceives you. Many will come in my name, claiming, "I am he," and will deceive many.
(Mark 13:5)

At that time if anyone says to you, "Look, here is the Christ!" or "Look, there he is!" do not believe it.
(Mark 13:21)

For false Christs and false prophets will appear and perform signs and miracles to deceive the elect — if that were possible. So be on your guard; I have told you everything ahead of time.
(Mark 13:22-23)

ANXIETY/ WORRY

See also:
Fear
Peace
Psalm 23
Refuge/Safety
Trust

Cast all your anxiety on him
because he cares for you.
(1 Peter 5:7)

Do not be anxious about anything, but in everything, by
prayer and petition, with thanksgiving, present your
requests to God. And the peace of God, which transcends
all understanding, will guard your hearts and your
minds in Christ Jesus.
(Philippians 4:6-7)

Do not fret — it leads only to evil.
(Psalm 37:8)

Martha, Martha, the Lord answered, *you are worried and
upset about many things, but only one thing is needed. Mary
has chosen what is better, and it will not be taken away from
her.*
(Luke 10:41-42)

For God did not give us a spirit of timidity, but a spirit of
power, of love and of self-discipline.
(2 Timothy 1:7)

*Who of you by worrying can add a single hour to his life?
Since you cannot do this very little thing, why do you worry
about the rest?*
(Luke 12:25-26)

An anxious heart weighs a man down, but a kind word
cheers him up.
(Proverbs 12:25)

Cast your cares on the LORD and he will sustain you; he will never let the righteous fall.
(Psalm 55:22)

When anxiety was great within me, your consolation brought joy to my soul.
(Psalm 94:19)

Search me, O God, and know my heart; test me and know my anxious thoughts. See if there is any offensive way in me, and lead me in the way everlasting.
(Psalm 139:23-24)

Therefore I tell you, do not worry about your life, what you will eat; or about your body, what you will wear. Life is more than food and the body more than clothes.
(Luke 12:22-23)

And why do you worry about clothes? See how the lilies of the field grow. They do not labor or spin. Yet I tell you that not even Solomon in all his splendor was dressed like one of these.
(Matthew 6:28-29)

So do not worry, saying "What shall we eat?" or "What shall we drink?" or "What shall we wear?" For the pagans run after all these things, and your heavenly Father knows that you need them.
(Matthew 6:31-32)

A man cannot discover anything about his future.
(Ecclesiastes 7:14)

Therefore do not worry about tomorrow, for tomorrow will worry about itself. Each day has enough trouble of its own.
(Matthew 6:34)

ARGUMENTATIVE

See also:
Communication
Marriage
 Guidance
Peace

I appeal to you, brothers, in the name of our Lord Jesus Christ, that all of you agree with one another so that there may be no divisions among you and that you may be perfectly united in mind and thought.
(1 Corinthians 1:10)

Don't have anything to do with foolish and stupid arguments, because you know they produce quarrels. And the Lord's servant must not quarrel; instead, he must be kind to everyone, able to teach, not resentful.
(2 Timothy 2:23-24)

Do everything without complaining or arguing, so that you may become blameless and pure, children of God without fault in a crooked and depraved generation, in which you shine like stars in the universe as you hold out the word of life.
(Philippians 2:14-16)

BACKSLIDING

See also:
Complacent
Denial
Doubt
Evil, Resisting
Repent
Sin, Consequences Of
Temptation
Unbelief

So, if you think you are standing firm, be careful that you don't fall!
(1 Corinthians 10:12)

If you do not stand firm in your faith, you will not stand at all.
(Isaiah 7:9)

But as for me, my feet had almost slipped; I had nearly lost my foothold. For I envied the arrogant when I saw the prosperity of the wicked.
(Psalm 73:2-3)

Therefore, my dear brothers, stand firm. Let nothing move you. Always give yourselves fully to the Lord, because you know that your labor in the Lord is not in vain.
(1 Corinthians 15:58)

We have come to share in Christ if we hold firmly till the end the confidence we had at first.
(Hebrews 3:14)

Let your eyes look straight ahead, fix your gaze directly before you. Make level paths for your feet and take only ways that are firm. Do not swerve to the right or the left; keep your foot from evil.
(Proverbs 4:25-27)

Return, faithless people; I will cure you of backsliding. Yes, we will come to you for you are the LORD our God.
(Jeremiah 3:22)

"Your wickedness will punish you; your backsliding will rebuke you. Consider then and realize how evil and bitter it is for you when you forsake the LORD your God and have no awe of me," declares the Lord, the LORD Almighty.
(Jeremiah 2:19)

Can papyrus grow tall where there is no marsh? Can reeds thrive without water? While still growing and uncut, they wither more quickly than grass. Such is the destiny of all who forget God; so perishes the hope of the godless.
(Job 8:11-13)

Some people are like seed along the path, where the word is sown. As soon as they hear it, Satan comes and takes away the word that was sown in them.
(Mark 4:15)

Still others, like seed sown among thorns, hear the word; but the worries of this life, the deceitfulness of wealth and the desires for other things come in and choke the word, making it unfruitful.
(Mark 4:18-19)

Cursed is the one who trusts in man, who depends on flesh for his strength and whose heart turns away from the LORD.
(Jeremiah 17:5)

Restore to me the joy of your salvation and grant me a willing spirit, to sustain me.
(Psalm 51:12)

Then I will teach transgressors your ways, and sinners will turn back to you.
(Psalm 51:13)

BELIEF

See also:
Born Again
Eternal Life
Faith
Salvation
Trust

Give ear and come to me; hear me,
that your soul may live.
(Isaiah 55:3)

Believe in the Lord Jesus, and you will
be saved — you and your household.
(Acts 16:31)

I tell you the truth, he who believes has everlasting life.
(John 6:47)

Who is it that overcomes the world? Only he who believes that Jesus is the Son of God.
(1 John 5:5)

See to it, brothers, that none of you has a sinful, unbelieving heart that turns away from the living God.
(Hebrews 3:12)

*He who belongs to God hears what God says. The reason you
do not hear is that you do not belong to God.*
(John 8:47)

We did not follow cleverly invented stories when we told
you about the power and coming of our Lord Jesus
Christ, but we were eyewitness of his majesty.
(2 Peter 1:16)

Everyone who believes that Jesus is the Christ is born of
God, and everyone who loves the father loves his child as
well.
(1 John 5:1)

If you believed Moses, you would believe me, for he wrote about me.
(John 5:46)

Do not believe me unless I do what my Father does. But if I do it, even though you do not believe me, believe the miracles, that you may know and understand that the Father is in me, and I in the Father.
(John 10:37-38)

What must we do to do the works God requires? Jesus answered, *The work of God is this: to believe in the one he has sent.*
(John 6:28-29)

And this is his command: to believe in the name of his Son, Jesus Christ, and to love one another as he commanded us.
(1 John 3:23)

When a man believes in me, he does not believe in me only, but in the one who sent me. When he looks at me, he sees the one who sent me.
(John 12:44-45)

Through him you believe in God, who raised him from the dead and glorified him, and so your faith and hope are in God.
(1 Peter 1:21)

For my Father's will is that everyone who looks to the Son and believes in him shall have eternal life, and I will raise him up at the last day.
(John 6:40)

In your hearts set apart Christ as Lord.
(1 Peter 3:15)

*Because you have seen me, you have believed; blessed are those
who have not seen and yet have believed.*
(John 20:29)

Though you have not seen him, you love him; and even
though you do not see him now, you believe in him and
are filled with an inexpressible and glorious joy, for you
are receiving the goal of your faith, the salvation of your
souls.
(1 Peter 1:8-9)

Yet I am not ashamed, because I know whom I have
believed, and am convinced that he is able to guard what
I have entrusted to him for that day.
(2 Timothy 1:12)

It is written: "I believed; therefore I have spoken." With
that same spirit of faith we also believe and therefore
speak, because we know that the one who raised the
Lord Jesus from the dead will also raise us with Jesus and
present us with you in his presence.
(2 Corinthians 4:13-14)

Yet to all who received him, to those who believed in his
name, he gave the right to become children of God.
(John 1:12)

Jesus did many other miraculous signs in the presence of
his disciples, which are not recorded in this book. But
these are written that you may believe that Jesus is the
Christ, the Son of God, and that by believing you may
have life in his name.
(John 20:30-32)

*Whoever believes and is baptized will be saved, but whoever
does not believe will be condemned.*
(Mark 16:16)

BLASPHEMY

See also:
Forgiveness
Sin, Consequences Of

And everyone who speaks a word against the Son of Man will be forgiven, but anyone who blasphemes against the Holy Spirit will not be forgiven.
(Luke 12:10)

I tell you the truth, all the sins and blasphemies of men will be forgiven them. But whoever blasphemes against the Holy Spirit will never be forgiven; he is guilty of an eternal sin.
(Mark 3:28-29)

BLESSINGS

See also:
Eternal Life
Joy
Praise Him
Prayer, Answers To
Salvation
Sing Praises
Thankful

The LORD has done great things
for us, and we are filled with joy.
(Psalm 126:3)

From the fullness of his grace
we have all received one
blessing after another.
(John 1:16)

The lions may grow weak and hungry, but those who
seek the LORD lack no good thing.
(Psalm 34:10)

You prepare a table before me in the presence of my enemies. You anoint my head with oil; my cup overflows.
(Psalm 23:5)

He fulfills the desires of those who fear him; he hears
their cry and saves them.
(Psalm 145:19)

Now he who supplies seed to the sower and bread for
food will also supply and increase your store of seed and
will enlarge the harvest of your righteousness.
(2 Corinthians 9:10)

And my God will meet all your needs according to his
glorious riches in Christ Jesus.
(Philippians 4:19)

If you pay attention to these laws and are careful to follow
them, then the LORD your God will keep his covenant of love
with you, as he swore to your forefathers. He will love you
and bless you and increase your numbers.
(Deuteronomy 7:12-13)

The wages of the righteous bring them life, but the income of the wicked brings them punishment.
(Proverbs 10:16)

When God gives any man wealth and possessions, and enables him to enjoy them, to accept his lot and be happy in his work — this is a gift of God. He seldom reflects on the days of his life, because God keeps him occupied with gladness of heart.
(Ecclesiastes 5:19-20)

How great is your goodness, which you have stored up for those who fear you, which you bestow in the sight of men on those who take refuge in you.
(Psalm 31:19)

Surely you will reward each person according to what he has done.
(Psalm 62:12)

May the LORD repay you for what you have done. May you be richly rewarded by the LORD, the God of Israel, under whose wings you have come to take refuge.
(Ruth 2:12)

All nations will be blessed through him, and they will call him blessed.
(Psalm 72:17)

For the LORD God is a sun and shield; the LORD bestows favor and honor; no good thing does he withhold from those whose walk is blameless.
(Psalm 84:11)

He who did not spare his own Son, but gave him up for us all — how will he not also, along with him, graciously give us all things?
(Romans 8:32)

May God be gracious to us and bless us and make his
face shine upon us.
(Psalm 67:1)

And God is able to make all grace abound to you, so that
in all things at all times, having all that you need, you
will abound in every good work.
(2 Corinthians 9:8)

Surely goodness and love will follow me all the days of
my life, and I will dwell in the house of the LORD forever.
(Psalm 23:6)

BOASTFUL

See also:
Conceit
God, All Powerful
God, Awesome
Humility
Intelligence
Mortal Man
Prejudice
Pride
Sinful Nature
Wisdom

Let him who boasts boast in the Lord.
(1 Corinthians 1:31)

For who makes you different from anyone else? What do you have that you did not receive? And if you did receive it, why do you boast as though you did not?
(1 Corinthians 4:7)

You boast and brag. All such boasting is evil.
(James 4:16)

May the LORD cut off all flattering lips and every boastful tongue that says, "We will triumph with our tongues; we own our lips — who is our master?"
(Psalm 12:3)

Why do you boast of evil, you mighty man? Why do you boast all day long, you who are a disgrace in the eyes of the God?
(Psalm 52:1)

Do not boast about tomorrow, for you do not know what a day may bring forth.
(Proverbs 27:1)

May I never boast except in the cross of our Lord Jesus Christ, through which the world has been crucified to me, and I to the world.
(Galatians 6:14)

Let him who boasts boast in the Lord.
(2 Corinthians 10:17)

BORN AGAIN

See also:
Belief
Faith
Holy Spirit
Holy Spirit, Pentecost
Repent

I tell you the truth, no one can see the kingdom of God unless he is born again.
(John 3:3)

I tell you the truth, no on can enter the kingdom of God unless he is born of water and the Spirit.
(John 3:5)

Flesh gives birth to flesh, but the Spirit gives birth to Spirit.
(John 3:6)

But if Christ is in you, your body is dead because of sin, yet your spirit is alive because of righteousness.
(Romans 8:10)

He who has the Son has life; he who does not have the Son of God does not have life.
(1 John 5:12)

Therefore, if anyone is in Christ, he is a new creation; the old has gone, the new has come!
(2 Corinthians 5:17)

For whoever wants to save his life will lose it, but whoever loses his life for me will find it.
(Matthew 16:25)

I have been crucified with Christ and I no longer live, but Christ lives in me.
(Galatians 2:20)

I die every day — I mean that, brothers — just as surely as I glory over you in Christ Jesus our Lord.
(1 Corinthians 15:31)

What you sow does not come to life unless it dies.
(1 Corinthians 15:36)

For we who are alive are always being given over to
death for Jesus' sake, so that his life may be revealed in
our mortal body.
(2 Corinthians 4:11)

We know that we have passed from death to life, because
we love our brothers.
(1 John 3:14)

No one who is born of God will continue to sin, because
God's seed remains in him; he cannot go on sinning,
because he has been born of God.
(1 John 3:9)

But because of his great love for us, God, who is rich in
mercy, made us alive with Christ even when we were
dead in transgressions.
(Ephesians 2:4-5)

By dying to what once bound us, we have been released
from the law so that we serve in the new way of the
Spirit, and not in the old way of the written code.
(Romans 7:6)

In the same way, count yourselves dead to sin but alive
to God in Christ Jesus.
(Romans 6:11)

For you have been born again, not of perishable seed, but of
imperishable, through the living and enduring word of God.
(1 Peter 1:23)

If we died with him, we will also live with him; if we
endure, we will also reign with him.
(2 Timothy 2:11-12)

CHILD ABUSE/ NEGLECT

See also:
Children
Lust
Sex, Perverted

No one is to approach any close relative to have sexual relations.
(Leviticus 18:6)

Do not have sexual relations with your son's daughter or your daughter's daughter; that would dishonor you.
(Leviticus 18:10)

Things that cause people to sin are bound to come, but woe to that person through whom they come.
(Luke 17:1)

It would be better for him to be thrown into the sea with a millstone tied around his neck than for him to cause one of these little ones to sin.
(Luke 17:2)

See that you do not look down on one of these little ones. For I tell you that their angels in heaven always see the face of my Father in heaven.
(Matthew 18:10)

Though my father and mother forsake me, the LORD will receive me.
(Psalm 27:10)

CHILDREN

See also:
Adolescent Guidance
Adolescent Rebellion
Child Abuse/Neglect
Parenting

*Whoever welcomes this little child
in my name welcomes me; and
whoever welcomes me welcomes the
one who sent me. For he who is least
among you all — he is the greatest.*
(Luke 9:48)

*I praise you, Father, Lord of heaven and earth, because you have
hidden these things from the wise and learned, and revealed them to
little children. Yes, Father, for this was your good pleasure.*
(Luke 10:21)

From the lips of children and infants you have ordained
praise.
(Psalm 8:2)

*Let the little children come to me, and do not hinder them, for
the kingdom of God belongs to such as these.*
(Mark 10:14)

*I tell you the truth, unless you change and become like little
children, you will never enter the kingdom of heaven.*
(Matthew 18:3)

*The greatest among you should be like the youngest, and the
one who rules like the one who serves.*
(Luke 22:26)

*Therefore, whoever humbles himself like this child is the great-
est in the kingdom of heaven.*
(Matthew 18:4)

*And whoever welcomes a little child like this in my name
welcomes me.*
(Matthew 18:5)

CHOSEN/ELECT

See also:
End Times
Plans

But you are a chosen people, a royal priesthood, a holy nation, a people belonging to God, that you may declare the praises of him who called you out of darkness into his wonderful light.
(1 Peter 2:9)

For he chose us in him before the creation of the world to be holy and blameless in his sight.
(Ephesians 1:4)

For we are God's workmanship, created in Christ Jesus to do good works, which God prepared in advance for us to do.
(Ephesians 2:10)

When the Gentiles heard this, they were glad and honored the word of the Lord; and all who were appointed for eternal life believed.
(Acts 13:48)

For those God foreknew he also predestined to be conformed to the likeness of his Son, that he might be the firstborn among many brothers.
(Romans 8:29)

And those he predestined, he also called; those he called, he also justified; those he justified, he also glorified.
(Romans 8:30)

But we ought always to thank God for you, brothers loved by the Lord, because from the beginning God chose you to be saved through the sanctifying work of the Spirit and through belief in the truth.
(2 Thessalonians 2:13)

And we know that in all things God works for the good of those who love him, who have been called according to his purpose.
(Romans 8:28)

For it is God who works in you to will and to act according to his good purpose.
(Philippians 2:13)

You did not choose me, but I chose you and appointed you to go and bear fruit—fruit that will last. Then the Father will give you whatever you ask in my name.
(John 15:16)

All that the Father gives me will come to me, and whoever comes to me I will never drive away.
(John 6:37)

No one can come to me unless the Father who sent me draws him, and I will raise him up at the last day.
(John 6:44)

If you belonged to the world, it would love you as its own. As it is, you do not belong to the world, but I have chosen you out of the world. That is why the world hates you.
(John 15:19)

For you granted him authority over all people that he might give eternal life to all those you have given him.
(John 17:2)

Make every effort to enter through the narrow door, because many, I tell you, will try to enter and will not be able to.
(Luke 13:24)

No one knows the Son except the Father, and no one knows the Father except the Son and those to whom the Son chooses to reveal him.
(Matthew 11:27)

Then the king told the attendants, "Tie him hand and foot, and throw him outside, into the darkness, where there will be weeping and gnashing of teeth." For many are invited, but few are chosen.
(Matthew 22:13-14)

They will see the Son of Man coming on the clouds of the sky, with power and great glory. And he will send his angels with a loud trumpet call, and they will gather his elect from the four winds, from one end of the heavens to the other.
(Matthew 24:30-31)

The things you planned for us no one can recount to you; were I to speak and tell of them, they would be too many to declare.
(Psalm 40:5)

CHRIST, DEATH OF

See also:
Christ, Mission Of
Christ, Resurrection Of
Christ, Sacrifice Of

He died for us so that, whether we are awake or asleep, we may live together with him.
(1 Thessalonians 5:10)

I am the good shepherd. The good shepherd lays down his life for the sheep.
(John 10:11)

He was oppressed and afflicted, yet he did not open his mouth; he was led like a lamb to slaughter, and as a sheep before her shearers is silent, so he did not open his mouth.
(Isaiah 53:7)

Yet it was the LORD's will to crush him and cause him to suffer, and though the LORD makes his life a guilt offering, he will see his offspring and prolong his days, and the will of the LORD will prosper in his hand.
(Isaiah 53:10)

I tell you the truth, you will weep and mourn while the world rejoices. You will grieve, but your grief will turn to joy.
(John 16:20)

From that time on Jesus began to explain to his disciples that he must go to Jerusalem and suffer many things at the hands of the elders, chief priests and teachers of the law, and that he must be killed and on the third day be raised to life.
(Matthew 16:21)

Father, the time has come. Glorify your Son, that your Son may glorify you.
(John 17:1)

They stripped him and put a scarlet robe on him, and then twisted together a crown of thorns and set it on his head. They put a staff in his right hand and knelt in front of him and mocked him. "Hail, king of the Jews!" they said.
(Matthew 27:28-29)

They spit on him, and took the staff and struck him on the head again and again.
(Matthew 27:30)

After they had mocked him, they took off the robe and put his own clothes on him. Then they led him away to crucify him.
(Matthew 27:31)

From the sixth hour until the ninth hour darkness came over all the land.
(Matthew 27:45)

About the ninth hour Jesus cried out in a loud voice, *Eloi, Eloi, lama sabachthani? — which means, My God, my God, why have you forsaken me?*
(Matthew 27:46)

Immediately one of them ran and got a sponge. He filled it with wine vinegar, put it on a stick, and offered it to Jesus to drink.
(Matthew 27:48)

And when Jesus had cried out again in a loud voice, he gave up his spirit.
(Matthew 27:50)

At that moment the curtain of the temple was torn in two from top to bottom. The earth shook and the rocks split.
(Matthew 27:51)

The tombs broke open and the bodies of many holy
people who had died were raised to life. They came out
of the tombs, and after Jesus' resurrection they went into
the holy city and appeared to many people.
(Matthew 27:52-53)

When the centurion and those with him who were
guarding Jesus saw the earthquake and all that had
happened, they were terrified, and exclaimed, "Surely he
was the Son of God."
(Matthew 27:54)

CHRIST, DIVINITY OF

See also:
Christ, Humanity Of
Christ, Identity Of
Christ, Personality Of

In the beginning was the Word, and the Word was with God, and the Word was God.
(John 1:1)

He was with God in the beginning.
(John 1:2)

Through him all things were made; without him nothing was made that has been made.
(John 1:3)

We have seen his glory, the glory of the One and Only, who came from the Father, full of grace and truth.
(John 1:14)

No one has ever seen God, but God the One and Only, who is at the Father's side, has made him know.
(John 1:18)

No one has ever gone into heaven except the one who came from heaven — the Son of Man.
(John 3:13)

The one who comes from above is above all.
(John 3:31)

For the one whom God has sent speaks the words of God, for God gives the Spirit without limit.
(John 3:34)

I tell you the truth, the Son can do nothing by himself; he can do only what he sees his Father doing, because whatever the Father does the Son also does.
(John 5:19)

For as the Father has life in himself, so he has granted the Son to have life in himself.
(John 5:26)

For the very work that the Father has given me to finish, and which I am doing, testifies that the Father has sent me.
(John 5:36)

And the Father who sent me has himself testified concerning me.
(John 5:37)

On him God the Father has placed his seal of approval.
(John 6:27)

No one has seen the Father except the one who is from God; only he has seen the Father.
(John 6:46)

In your own Law it is written that the testimony of two men is valid. I am one who testifies for myself; my other witness is the Father, who sent me.
(John 8:17)

You do not know me or my Father, Jesus replied. If you knew me, you would know my Father also.
(John 8:19)

But he who sent me is reliable, and what I have heard from him I tell the world.
(John 8:26)

When you have lifted up the Son of Man, then you will know that I am the one I claim to be and that I do nothing on my own but speak just what the Father has taught me.
(John 8:28)

I have not come on my own; but he sent me.
(John 8:42)

Though you do not know him, I know him. If I said I did not, I would be a liar like you, but I do know him and keep his word.
(John 8:55)

For I did not speak of my own accord, but the Father who sent me commanded me what to say and how to say it. I know that his command leads to eternal life. So whatever I say is just what the Father has told me to say.
(John 12:49-50)

You call me "Teacher" and "Lord," and rightly so, for that is what I am.
(John 13:13)

If you really knew me, you would know my Father as well. From now on, you do know him and have seen him.
(John 14:7)

Anyone who has seen me has seen the Father.
(John 14:9)

The words I say to you are not just my own. Rather, it is the Father, living in me, who is doing his work.
(John 14:10)

All that belongs to the Father is mine.
(John 16:15)

My kingdom is not of this world.
(John 18:36)

He is the true God and eternal life.
(1 John 5:20)

He was chosen before the creation of the world, but was revealed in these last times for your sake.
(1 Peter 1:20)

For he received honor and glory from God the Father when the voice came to him from the Majestic Glory, saying, "This is my Son, whom I love; with him I am well pleased."
(2 Peter 1:17)

That power is like the working of his mighty strength, which he exerted in Christ when he raised him from the dead and seated him at his right hand in the heavenly realms, far above all rule and authority, power and dominion, and every title that can be given, not only in the present age but also in the one to come.
(Ephesians 1:19-21)

So he became as much superior to the angels as the name he has inherited is superior to theirs.
(Hebrews 1:4)

You have loved righteousness and hated wickedness; therefore God, your God, has set you above your companions by anointing you with the oil of joy.
(Hebrews 1:9)

But from now on, the Son of Man will be seated at the right hand of the mighty God.
(Luke 22:69)

Therefore God exalted him to the highest place and gave him the name that is above every name, that at the name of Jesus every knee should bow, in heaven and on earth

and under the earth, and every tongue confess that Jesus Christ is Lord, to the glory of God the Father.
(Philippians 2:9-11)

Holy, holy, holy is the Lord God Almighty, who was, and is, and is to come.
(Revelation 4:8)

CHRIST, HUMANITY OF

See also:
Christ, Divinity Of
Christ, Identity Of
Christ, Personality Of

The Word became flesh and made his dwelling among us.
(John 1:14)

Today in the town of David a Savior has been born to you; he is Christ the Lord. This will be a sign to you: You will find a baby wrapped in cloths and lying in a manger.
(Luke 2:11-12)

But when the time had fully come, God sent his Son, born of a woman, born under law, to redeem those under law, that we might receive the full rights of sons.
(Galatians 4:4-5)

He had no beauty or majesty to attract us to him, nothing in his appearance that we should desire him.
(Isaiah 53:2)

He was in the world, and though the world was made through him, the world did not recognize him.
(John 1:10)

Since the children have flesh and blood, he too shared in their humanity so that by his death he might destroy him who holds the power of death — that is, the devil — and free those who all their lives were held slavery by the fear of death.
(Hebrews 2:14-15)

Because he himself suffered when he was tempted, he is able to help those who are being tempted.
(Hebrews 2:18)

For we do not have a high priest who is unable to sympathize with our weaknesses, but we have one who has been tempted in every way, just as we are — yet was without sin.
(Hebrews 4:15)

For forty days he was tempted by the devil. He ate nothing during those days, and at the end of them he was hungry.
(Luke 4:2)

During the days of Jesus' life on earth, he offered up prayers and petitions with loud cries and tears to the one who could save him from death, and he was heard because of his reverent submission.
(Hebrews 5:7)

My soul is overwhelmed with sorrow to the point of death, he said to them. *Stay here and keep watch.*
(Mark 14:34)

Jesus said, *I am thirsty.*
(John 19:28)

When he had received the drink, Jesus said, *It is finished.* With that, he bowed his head and gave up his spirit.
(John 19:30)

And being found in appearance as a man, he humbled himself and became obedient to death — even death on a cross!
(Philippians 2:8)

CHRIST, IDENTITY OF

See also:
Christ, Divinity Of
Christ, Humanity Of
Christ, Personality Of

I am the First and the Last.
(Revelation 1:17)

I am the Alpha and the Omega, says the Lord God, *who is, and who was, and who is to come, the Almighty.*
(Revelation 1:8)

Before Abraham was born, I am!
(John 8:58)

I and the Father are one.
(John 10:30)

I am in my Father, and you are in me, and I am in you.
(John 14:20)

I am the Root and the Offspring of David, and the bright Morning Star.
(Revelation 22:16)

I am the light of the world. Whoever follows me will never walk in darkness, but will have the light of life.
(John 8:12)

I am the gate; whoever enters through me will be saved.
(John 10:9)

I am the way and the truth and the life. No one comes to the Father except through me.
(John 14:6)

I am the bread of life.
(John 6:48)

I am the living bread that came down from heaven. If anyone eats of this bread, he will live forever.
(John 6:51)

I am the good shepherd; I know my sheep and my sheep know me — just as the Father knows me and I know the Father — and I lay down my life for the sheep.
(John 10:14-15)

I am the true vine, and my Father is the gardener. He cuts off every branch in me that bears no fruit, while every branch that does bear fruit he prunes so that it will be even more fruitful.
(John 15:1)

I am among you as one who serves.
(Luke 22:27)

I am not here on my own, but he who sent me is true. You do not know him, but I know him because I am from him and he sent me.
(John 7:28-29)

You are from below; I am from above. You are of this world; I am not of this world.
(John 8:23)

I am the Living One; I was dead, and behold I am alive for ever and ever! And I hold the keys of death and Hades.
(Revelation 1:18)

I am the resurrection and the life. He who believes in me will live, even though he dies; and whoever lives and believes in me will never die.
(John 11:25-26)

CHRIST, MISSION OF

See also:
Christ, Death Of
Christ, Resurrection Of
Christ, Sacrifice Of
Salvation

She will give birth to a son, and you are to give him the name Jesus, because he will save his people from their sins.
(Matthew 1:21)

This is love: not that we loved God, but that he loved us and sent his Son as an atoning sacrifice for our sins.
(1 John 4:10)

For Christ died for sins once for all, the righteous for the unrighteous, to bring you to God. He was put to death in the body but made alive by the Spirit.
(1 Peter 3:18)

He appeared so that he might take away our sins.
(1 John 3:5)

Look, the Lamb of God, who takes away the sin of the world!
(John 1:29)

And he died for all, that those who live should no longer live for themselves but for him who died for them and was raised again.
(2 Corinthians 5:15)

He was delivered over to death for our sins and was raised to life for our justification.
(Romans 4:25)

By his power God raised the Lord from the dead, and he will raise us also.
(1 Corinthians 6:14)

After he had provided purification for sins, he sat down at the right hand of the Majesty in heaven.
(Hebrews 1:3)

God exalted him to his own right hand as Prince and Savior that he might give repentance and forgiveness of sins to Israel.
(Acts 5:31)

But we also rejoice in God through our Lord Jesus Christ, through whom we have now received reconciliation.
(Romans 5:11)

In him and through faith in him we may approach God with freedom and confidence.
(Ephesians 3:12)

The Son of man must be lifted up, that everyone who believes in him may have eternal life.
(John 3:14-15)

I have come that they may have life, and have it to the full.
(John 10:10)

I have come into the world as a light, so that no one who believes in me should stay in darkness.
(John 12:46)

But I, when I am lifted up from the earth, will draw all men to myself.
(John 12:32)

Since the children have flesh and blood, he too shared in their humanity so that by his death he might destroy him who holds the power of death — that is, the devil — and free those who all their lives were held in slavery by their fear of death.
(Hebrews 2:14-15)

Do not think that I have come to abolish the Law or the Prophets; I have not come to abolish them but to fulfill them.
(Matthew 5:17)

But when the time had fully come, God sent his Son, born of a woman, born under law, to redeem those under law, that we might receive the full rights of sons.
(Galatians 4:4-5)

Christ is the end of the law so that there may be righteousness for everyone who believes.
(Romans 10:4)

I have not come to call the righteous, but sinners.
(Matthew 9:13)

I was sent only to the lost sheep of Israel.
(Matthew 15:24)

Do not suppose that I have come to bring peace to the earth. I did not come to bring peace, but a sword.
(Matthew 10:34)

For I have come to turn "a man against his father, a daughter against her mother, a daughter-in-law against her mother-in-law — a man's enemies will be the members of his own household."
(Matthew 10:35-36)

"You are a king, then!" said Pilate. Jesus answered, *You are right in saying I am a king. In fact, for this reason I was born, and for this I came into the world, to testify to the truth. Everyone on the side of truth listens to me.*
(John 18:37)

I must preach the good news of the kingdom of God to the other towns also, because that is why I was sent.
(Luke 4:43)

The Son of Man did not come to be served, but to serve, and to give his life as a ransom for many.
(Mark 10:45)

Jesus, who rescues us from the coming wrath.
(1 Thessalonians 1:10)

My food, said Jesus, is to do the will of him who sent me and to finish his work.
(John 4:34)

I have brought you glory on earth by completing the work you gave me to do.
(John 17:4)

To him who is able to keep you from falling and to present you before his glorious presence without fault and with great joy — to the only God our Savior be glory, majesty, power and authority, through Jesus Christ our Lord, before all ages, now and forevermore! Amen.
(Jude 1:24-25)

CHRIST, PERSONALITY OF

See also:
Christ, Divinity Of
Christ, Humanity Of
Christ, Identity Of

And in him is no sin.
(1 John 3:5)

He committed no sin, and no deceit was found in his mouth.
(1 Peter 2:22)

We do not have a high priest who is unable to sympathize with our weaknesses, but we have one who has been tempted in every way, just as we are — yet was without sin.
(Hebrews 4:15)

Take my yoke upon you and learn from me, for I am gentle and humble in heart, and will find rest for your souls.
(Matthew 11:29)

The one who sent me is with me; he has not left me alone, for I always do what pleases him.
(John 8:29)

I am not seeking glory for myself; but there is one who seeks it, and he is the judge.
(John 8:50)

By the meekness and gentleness of Christ, I appeal to you.
(2 Corinthians 10:1)

I have compassion for these people; they have already been with me three days and have nothing to eat. If I send them home hungry, they will collapse on the way, because some of them have come a long distance.
(Mark 8:2-3)

When the Lord saw her, his heart went out to her and he
said, *Don't cry.*
(Luke 7:13)

When Jesus saw her weeping, and the Jews who had
come along with her also weeping, he was deeply moved
in spirit and troubled.
(John 11:33)

Jesus wept.
(John 11:35)

But for that very reason I was shown mercy so that in me,
the worst of sinners, Christ Jesus might display his un-
limited patience as an example for those who would
believe on him and receive eternal life.
(1 Timothy 1:16)

Then he entered the temple area and began driving out
those who were selling.
(Luke 19:45)

So he made a whip out of cords, and drove all from the
temple area, both sheep and cattle; he scattered the coins
of the money changers and overturned their tables.
(John 2:15)

"No one ever spoke the way this man does," the guards
declared.
(John 7:46)

*For she came from the ends of the earth to listen to Solomon's
wisdom, and now one greater than Solomon is here...and now
one greater than Jonah is here.*
(Luke 11:31-32)

All the people hung on his words.
(Luke 19:48)

Listen and understand. What goes into a man's mouth does not make him "unclean," but what comes out of his mouth, that is what makes him "unclean."
(Matthew 15:10)

But I tell you: Love your enemies and pray for those who persecute you.
(Matthew 5:44)

But I tell you that anyone who looks at a woman lustfully has already committed adultery with her in his heart.
(Matthew 5:28)

The Son of Man did not come to be served, but to serve, and to give his life as a ransom for many.
(Matthew 20:28)

Therefore I tell you, do not worry about your life, what you will eat or drink; or about your body, what you will wear. Is not life more important than food, and the body more important than clothes?
(Matthew 6:25)

He poured water into a basin and began to wash his disciples' feet, drying them with the towel that was wrapped around him.
(John 13:5)

At that time Jesus, full of joy through the Holy Spirit, said, *I praise you, Father, Lord of heaven and earth, because you have hidden these things from the wise and learned, and revealed them to little children. Yes, Father, for this was your good pleasure.*
(Luke 10:21)

This man welcomes sinners and eats with them.
(Luke 15:2)

All the people saw this and began to mutter, "He has gone to be the guest of a 'sinner.'"
(Luke 19:7)

Sit here while I pray.
(Mark 14:32)

And being in anguish, he prayed more earnestly, and his sweat was like drops of blood falling to the ground.
(Luke 22:44)

Jesus Christ is the same yesterday and today and forever.
(Hebrews 13:8)

CHRIST, RESURRECTION OF

See also:
Christ, Death Of
Christ, Mission Of
Christ, Sacrifice Of

In a little while you will see me no more, and then after a little while you will see me.
(John 16:16)

This is what is written: The Christ will suffer and rise from the dead on the third day, and repentance and forgiveness of sins will be preached in his name to all nations, beginning at Jerusalem.
(Luke 24:46-47)

God raised him from the dead, freeing him from the agony of death, because it was impossible for death to keep its hold on him.
(Acts 2:24)

Why do you look for the living among the dead?
(Luke 24:5)

He is not here; he has risen!
(Luke 24:6)

God raised him from the dead, and for many days he was seen by those who had traveled with him from Galilee to Jerusalem.
(Acts 13:30-31)

Why are you troubled, and why do doubts rise in your minds? Look at my hands and my feet. It is I myself! Touch me and see; a ghost does not have flesh and bones, as you see I have.
(Luke 24:38-39)

After his suffering, he showed himself to these men and gave many convincing proofs that he was alive. He appeared to them over a period of forty days and spoke about the kingdom of God.
(Acts 1:3)

When he had led them out to the vicinity of Bethany, he lifted up his hands and blessed them. While he was blessing them, he left them and was taken up into heaven.
(Luke 24:50-51)

I am the Living One; I was dead, and behold I am alive for ever and ever! And I hold the keys of death and Hades.
(Revelation 1:18)

And if Christ has not been raised, our preaching is useless and so is your faith.
(1 Corinthians 15:14)

For we know that since Christ was raised from the dead, he cannot die again; death no longer has mastery over him. The death he died, he died to sin once for all; but the life he lives, he lives to God.
(Romans 6:9-10)

Praise be to the God and Father of our Lord Jesus Christ! In his great mercy he has given us new birth into a living hope through the resurrection of Jesus Christ from the dead.
(1 Peter 1:3)

I want to know Christ and the power of his resurrection and the fellowship of sharing in his sufferings, becoming like him in his death, and so, somehow, to attain to the resurrection from the dead.
(Philippians 3:10-11)

We believe that Jesus died and rose again and so we believe that God will bring with Jesus those who have fallen asleep in him.
(1 Thessalonians 4:14)

With great power the apostles continued to testify to the resurrection of the Lord Jesus, and much grace was upon them all.
(Acts 4:33)

CHRIST, SACRIFICE OF

See also:
Christ, Death Of
Christ, Mission Of
Christ, Resurrection Of
Salvation

He himself bore our sins in his body on the tree, so that we might die to sins and live for righteousness; by his wounds you have been healed.
(1 Peter 2:24)

He was put to death in the body but made alive by the Spirit.
(1 Peter 3:18)

God made him who had no sin to be sin for us, so that in him we might become the righteousness of God.
(2 Corinthians 5:21)

Christ redeemed us from the curse of the law by becoming a curse for us, for it is written: "Cursed is everyone who is hung on a tree."
(Galatians 3:13)

He suffered death, so that by the grace of God he might taste death for everyone.
(Hebrews 2:9)

But he was pierced for our transgressions, he was crushed for our iniquities; the punishment that brought us peace was upon him, and by his wounds we are healed.
(Isaiah 53:5)

They hated me without reason.
(John 15:25)

He was delivered over to death for our sins and was
raised to life for our justification.
(Romans 4:25)

The death he died, he died to sin once for all; but the life
he lives, he lives to God.
(Romans 6:10)

CHURCH

See also:
Friendship
Gifts, Spiritual
Love, For Others
Occupation/Job/Work
Persecution
Witness
Worship

The body is a unit, though it is made up of many parts; and though all its parts are many, they form one body. So it is with Christ.
(1 Corinthians 12:12)

And he is the head of the body, the church.
(Colossians 1:18)

And God placed all things under his feet and appointed him to be head over everything for the church, which is his body, the fullness of him who fills everything in every way.
(Ephesians 1:22-23)

But God has combined the members of the body and has given greater honor to the parts that lacked it, so that there should be no division in the body, but that its parts should have equal concern for each other.
(1 Corinthians 12:24-25)

Now you are the body of Christ, and each one of you is a part of it.
(1 Corinthians 12:27)

If one part suffers, every part suffers with it; if one part is honored, every part rejoices with it.
(1 Corinthians 12:26)

Holy Father, protect them by the power of your name — the name you gave me — so that they may be one as we are one.
(John 17:11)

Just as each of us has one body with many members, and these members do not all have the same function, so in Christ we who are many form one body, and each member belongs to all the others.
(Romans 12:4-5)

May the God who gives endurance and encouragement give you a spirit of unity among yourselves as you follow Christ Jesus, so that with one heart and mouth you may glorify the God and father of our Lord Jesus Christ.
(Romans 15:5-6)

And in the church God has appointed first of all apostles, second prophets, third teachers, then workers of miracles, also those having gifts of healing, those able to help others, those with gifts of administration, and those speaking in different kinds of tongues.
(1 Corinthians 12:28)

Show proper respect to everyone: Love the brotherhood of believers, fear God, honor the king.
(1 Peter 2:17)

Encourage one another and build each other up.
(1 Thessalonians 5:11)

All the believers were one in heart and mind. No one claimed that any of his possessions was his own, but they shared everything they had.
(Acts 4:32)

There were no needy persons among them. For from time to time those who owned lands or houses sold them, brought the money from the sales and put it at the apostles' feet, and it was distributed to anyone as he had need.
(Acts 4:34-35)

Therefore, as we have opportunity, let us do good to all people, especially to those who belong to the family of believers.
(Galatians 6:10)

But encourage one another daily, as long as it is called Today, so that none of you may be hardened by sin's deceitfulness.
(Hebrews 3:13)

And let us consider how we may spur one another on toward love and good deeds.
(Hebrews 10:24)

And do not forget to do good and to share with others, for with such sacrifices God is pleased.
(Hebrews 13:16)

Live in harmony with one another.
(Romans 12:16)

CITIZENSHIP

See also:
God, All Powerful

Obey your leaders and submit to their authority.
(Hebrews 13:17)

Submit yourselves for the Lord's sake to every authority instituted among men.
(1 Peter 2:13)

The authorities that exist have been established by God.
(Romans 13:1)

He who rebels against the authority is rebelling against what God has instituted, and those who do so will bring judgment on themselves.
(Romans 13:2)

For rulers hold no terror for those who do right, but for those who do wrong. Do you want to be free from fear of the one in authority? Then do what is right and he will commend you.
(Romans 13:3)

For he is God's servant to do you good. But if you do wrong, be afraid, for he does not bear the sword for nothing. He is God's servant, an agent of wrath to bring punishment on the wrongdoer.
(Romans 13:4)

Therefore, it is necessary to submit to authorities, not only because of possible punishment but also because of conscience.
(Romans 13:5)

This is why you pay taxes, for the authorities are God's servants, who give their full time to governing.
(Romans 13:6)

Give everyone what you owe him: If you owe taxes, pay taxes; if revenue, then revenue; if respect, then respect; if honor, then honor.
(Romans 13:7)

Give to Caesar what is Caesar's and to God what is God's.
(Mark 12:17)

But so that we may not offend them, go to the lake and throw out your line. Take the first fish you catch; open its mouth and you will find a four-drachma coin. Take it and give it to them for my tax and yours.
(Matthew 17:27)

Remind the people to be subject to rulers and authorities, to be obedient, to be ready to do whatever is good, to slander no one, to be peaceable and considerate, and to show true humility toward all men.
(Titus 3:1-2)

COMMANDMENTS

See also:
Action
Disobedience
Love, For Christ
Obedience
Ten Commandments
Truth

I open my mouth and pant,
longing for your commands.
(Psalm 119:131)

The ordinances of the LORD are
sure and altogether righteous.
(Psalm 19:9)

I have chosen the way of truth; I have set my heart on
your laws.
(Psalm 119:30)

I have run in the path of your commands, for you have
set my heart free.
(Psalm 119:32)

All the ways of the LORD are loving and faithful for those
who keep the demands of his covenant.
(Psalm 25:10)

Direct me in the path of your commands, for there I find
delight.
(Psalm 119:35)

Give me understanding, and I will keep your law and
obey it with all my heart.
(Psalm 119:34)

Teach me, O LORD, to follow your decrees; then I will
keep them to the end.
(Psalm 119:33)

COMMUNICATION

See also:
Argumentative
Gossip
Lying
Marriage Guidance
Slander
Swearing

If anyone speaks, he should do
it as one speaking the very
words of God.
(1 Peter 4:11)

The tongue has the power of life
and death.
(Proverbs 18:21)

*Men will have to give account on the day of judgment for every
careless word they have spoken.*
(Matthew 12:36)

He who guards his lips guards his life, but he who speaks
rashly will come to ruin.
(Proverbs 13:3)

With the tongue we praise our Lord and Father, and with
it we curse men, who have been made in God's likeness.
Out of the same mouth come praise and cursing.
(James 3:9-10)

The mouth of the righteous is a fountain of life, but
violence overwhelms the mouth of the wicked.
(Proverbs 10:11)

The lips of the righteous nourish many, but fools die for
lack of judgment.
(Proverbs 10:21)

I have resolved that my mouth will not sin.
(Psalm 17:3)

From the fruit of his lips a man is filled with good things
as surely as the work of his hands rewards him.
(Proverbs 12:14)

From the fruit of his mouth a man's stomach is filled;
with the harvest from his lips he is satisfied.
(Proverbs 18:20)

The quiet words of the wise are more to be heeded than
the shouts of a ruler of fools.
(Ecclesiastes 9:17)

Through patience a ruler can be persuaded, and a gentle
tongue can break a bone.
(Proverbs 25:15)

The tongue of the wise commends knowledge, but the
mouth of the fool gushes folly.
(Proverbs 15:2)

No man can tame the tongue. It is a restless evil, full of
deadly poison.
(James 3:8)

Reckless words pierce like a sword, but the tongue of the
wise brings healing.
(Proverbs 12:18)

You love every harmful word, O you deceitful tongue!
(Psalm 52:4)

The words of the wicked lie in wait for blood, but the
speech of the upright rescues them.
(Proverbs 12:6)

The heart of the righteous weighs its answers, but the
mouth of the wicked gushes evil.
(Proverbs 15:28)

Do you see a man who speaks in haste? There is more hope for a fool than for him.
(Proverbs 29:20)

He who guards his mouth and his tongue keeps himself from calamity.
(Proverbs 21:23)

Even a fool is thought wise if he keeps silent, and discerning if he holds his tongue.
(Proverbs 17:28)

Set a guard over my mouth, O LORD; keep watch over the door of my lips.
(Psalm 141:3)

For by your words you will be acquitted, and by your words you will be condemned.
(Matthew 12:37)

COMMUNION

See also:
Christ, Death Of
Christ, Mission Of
Christ, Resurrection Of

*Just as the living Father sent me and
I live because of the Father, so the
one who feeds on me will live because of me.*
(John 6:57)

The Lord Jesus, on the night he was betrayed, took bread,
and when he had given thanks, he broke it and said, *This
is my body, which is for you; do this in remembrance of me.*
(1 Corinthians 11:23-24)

In the same way, after supper he took the cup, saying,
*This cup is the new covenant in my blood; do this, whenever
you drink it, in remembrance of me.*
(1 Corinthians 11:25)

For whenever you eat this bread and drink this cup, you
proclaim the Lord's death until he comes.
(1 Corinthians 11:26)

 Therefore, whoever eats the bread or drinks the cup of
the Lord in an unworthy manner will be guilty of sinning
against the body and blood of the Lord.
(1 Corinthians 11:27)

A man ought to examine himself before he eats of the
bread and drinks of the cup.
(1 Corinthians 11:28)

For anyone who eats and drinks without recognizing the
body of the Lord eats and drinks judgment on himself.
(1 Corinthians 11:29)

Is not the cup of thanksgiving for which we give thanks a participation in the blood of Christ? And is not the bread that we break a participation in the body of Christ?
(1 Corinthians 10:16)

I tell you the truth, unless you eat the flesh of the Son of Man and drink his blood, you have no life in you.
(John 6:53)

Whoever eats my flesh and drinks my blood has eternal life, and I will raise him up at the last day.
(John 6:54)

COMPLACENT

See also:
Backsliding
End Times
Evil, Resisting
Repent
Second Coming
Temptation

The complacency of fools will destroy them.
(Proverbs 1:32)

When the Son of Man comes, will he find faith on the earth?
(Luke 18:8)

For the Son of Man is going to come in his Father's glory with his angels, and then he will reward each person according to what he has done.
(Matthew 16:27)

Be careful, or your hearts will be weighed down with dissipation, drunkenness and the anxieties of life, and that day will close on you unexpectedly like a trap.
(Luke 21:34)

That servant who knows his master's will and does not get ready or does not do what his master wants will be beaten with many blows.
(Luke 12:47)

What I say to you, I say to everyone: "Watch!"
(Mark 13:37)

The day of the Lord will come like a thief in the night.
(1 Thessalonians 5:2)

So then, let us not be like others, who are asleep, but let us be alert and self-controlled.
(1 Thessalonians 5:6)

The night is nearly over; the day is almost here. So let us put aside the deeds of darkness and put on the armor of light.
(Romans 13:12)

You ought to live holy and godly lives as you look forward to the day of God and speed its coming.
(2 Peter 3:11-12)

It will be good for those servants whose master finds them watching when he comes.
(Luke 12:37)

You must also be ready, because the Son of Man will come at an hour when you do not expect him.
(Luke 12:40)

Therefore keep watch, because you do not know the day or the hour.
(Matthew 25:13)

No one knows about that day or hour, not even the angels in heaven, nor the Son, but only the Father.
(Mark 13:32)

Be always on watch, and pray that you may be able to escape all that is about to happen, and that you may be able to stand before the Son of Man.
(Luke 21:36)

There is a judge for the one who rejects me and does not accept my words; that very word which I spoke will condemn him at the last day.
(John 12:48)

The hour has come for you to wake up from your slumber, because our salvation is nearer now than when we first believed.
(Romans 13:11)

I am coming soon. Hold on to what you have, so that no one will take your crown.
(Revelation 3:11)

Behold, I come like a thief! Blessed is he who stays awake.
(Revelation 16:15)

Yes, I am coming soon.
(Revelation 22:20)

CONCEIT

If anyone thinks he is something when he is nothing, he deceives himself.
(Galatians 6:3)

If you have played the fool and exalted yourself, or if you have planned evil, clap your hand over your mouth!
(Proverbs 30:32)

It is not good to eat too much honey, nor is it honorable to seek one's own honor.
(Proverbs 25:27)

Do not think of yourself more highly than you ought, but rather think of yourself with sober judgment, in accordance with the measure of faith God has given you.
(Romans 12:3)

For it is not the one who commends himself who is approved, but the one whom the Lord commends.
(2 Corinthians 10:18)

Since we live by the Spirit, let us keep in step with the Spirit. Let us not become conceited, provoking and envying each other.
(Galatians 5:25-26)

For they loved praise from men more than praise from God.
(John 12:43)

Do not be wise in your own eyes; fear the LORD and shun evil.
(Proverbs 3:7)

For in his own eyes he flatters himself too much to detect or hate his sin.
(Psalm 36:2)

Do not be proud, but be willing to associate with people of low position. Do not be conceited.
(Romans 12:16)

CONFESSION

See also:
Eternal Life
Forgiveness
Prayer, How To
Prayer, Hindrance To

He who conceals his sins does
not prosper, but whoever
confesses and renounces them
finds mercy.
(Proverbs 28:13)

If we confess our sins, he is faithful and just and will forgive
us our sins and purify us from all unrighteousness.
(1 John 1:9)

For it is with your heart that you believe and are justified,
and it is with your mouth that you confess and are saved.
(Romans 10:10)

O LORD, we acknowledge our wickedness and the guilt of
our fathers; we have indeed sinned against you.
(Jeremiah 14:20)

We have sinned, even as our fathers did; we have done
wrong and acted wickedly.
(Psalm 106:6)

We have sinned and done wrong. We have been wicked
and have rebelled; we have turned away from your
commands and laws.
(Daniel 9:5)

I confess my iniquity; I am troubled by my sin.
(Psalm 38:18)

How many wrongs and sins have I committed? Show me
my offense and my sin.
(Job 13:23)

Then I acknowledged my sin to you and did not cover up my iniquity. I said, "I will confess my transgressions to the LORD" — and you forgave the guilt of my sin.
(Psalm 32:5)

I said, "O LORD, have mercy on me; heal me, for I have sinned against you."
(Psalm 41:4)

Confess your sins to each other and pray for each other so that you may be healed.
(James 5:16)

Take hold of eternal life to which you were called when you made your good confession in the presence of many witnesses.
(1 Timothy 6:12)

Have mercy on me, O God, according to your unfailing love; according to your great compassion blot out my transgressions. Wash away all my iniquity and cleanse me from my sin.
(Psalm 51:1-2)

CONFUSION

See also:
Scripture/Word
Seeking
Thinking, Healthy
Thinking, Unhealthy
Truth
Wisdom

As you do not know the path of the wind, or how the body is formed in a mother's womb, so you cannot understand the work of God, the Maker of all things.
(Ecclesiastes 11:5)

I do not concern myself **with great** matters or things too wonderful for me.
(Psalm 131:1)

A man's steps are directed by the LORD. How then can anyone understand his own way?
(Proverbs 20:24)

It is the glory of God to conceal a matter.
(Proverbs 25:2)

For we know in part and we prophesy in part, but when perfection comes, the imperfect disappears.
(1 Corinthians 13:9-10)

There is nothing concealed that will not be disclosed, or hidden that will not be made known.
(Luke 12:2)

Now we see but a poor reflection as in a mirror; then we shall see face to face. Now I know in part; then I shall know fully, even as I am fully known.
(1 Corinthians 13:12)

The statutes of the LORD are trustworthy, making wise the simple.
(Psalm 19:7)

The unfolding of your words gives light; it gives understanding to the simple.
(Psalm 119:130)

If any of you lacks wisdom, he should ask God, who gives generously to all without finding fault, and it will be given to him.
(James 1:5)

We know also that the Son of God has come and has given us understanding, so that we may know him who is true.
(1 John 5:20)

Jesus spoke the word to them, as much as they could understand.
(Mark 4:33)

He did not say anything to them without using a parable. But when he was alone with his own disciples, he explained everything.
(Mark 4:34)

If you hold to my teaching, you are really my disciples. Then you will know the truth, and the truth will set you free.
(John 8:31-32)

But the Counselor, the Holy Spirit, whom the Father will send in my name, will teach you all things and will remind you of everything I have said to you.
(John 14:26)

Grow in the grace and knowledge of our Lord and Savior Jesus Christ. To him be glory both now and forever! Amen.
(2 Peter 3:18)

DARKNESS

See also:
Backsliding
Complacent
Denial
Doubt
Evil, Resisting
Light
Sin, Consequences Of
Unbelief

The people walking in darkness have seen a great light; on those living in the land of the shadow of death a light has dawned.
(Isaiah 9:2)

The darkness is passing and the true light is already shining.
(1 John 2:8)

I have come into the world as a light, so that no one who believes in me should stay in darkness.
(John 12:46)

Light has come into the world, but men loved darkness instead of light because their deeds were evil.
(John 3:19)

The light shines in the darkness, but the darkness has not understood it.
(John 1:5)

He brought them out of darkness and deepest gloom and broke away their chains.
(Psalm 107:14)

For he has rescued us from the dominion of darkness and brought us into the kingdom of the Son he loves, in whom we have redemption, the forgiveness of sins.
(Colossians 1:13-14)

For you were once darkness, but now you are light in the Lord.
(Ephesians 5:8)

The path of the righteous is like the first gleam of dawn, shining ever brighter till the full light of day.
(Proverbs 4:18)

A man who walks by day will not stumble, for he sees by this world's light. It is when he walks by night that he stumbles, for he has no light.
(John 11:9-10)

But everything exposed by the light becomes visible, for it is light that makes everything visible.
(Ephesians 5:13-14)

For judgment I have come into this world, so that the blind will see and those who see will become blind.
(John 9:39)

But whoever lives by the truth comes into the light, so that it may be seen plainly that what he has done has been done through God.
(John 3:21)

You, O LORD, keep my light burning; my God turns my darkness into light.
(Psalm 18:28)

DEATH/DYING

See also:
Disaster
Grief
Heaven
Help
Hopeless
Mercy
Prayer, Answers To
Psalm 23
Sickness
Sorrow
Strength
Suffering
Weakness

For he must reign until he has put all his enemies under his feet. The last enemy to be destroyed is death.
(1 Corinthians 15:25-26)

I declare to you, brothers, that flesh and blood cannot inherit the kingdom of God, nor does the perishable inherit the imperishable.
(1 Corinthians 15:50)

Listen, I tell you a mystery: We will not all sleep, but we will all be changed--in a flash, in the twinkling of an eye, at the last trumpet.
(1 Corinthians 15:51-52)

Where, O death, is your victory? Where, O death, is your sting?
(1 Corinthians 15:55)

No man has power over the wind to contain it; so no one has power over the day of his death.
(Ecclesiastes 8:8)

I will ransom them from the power of the grave; I will redeem them from death. Where, O death, are your plagues? Where, O grave, is your destruction?
(Hosea 13:14)

Those who walk uprightly enter into peace; they find rest as they lie in death.
(Isaiah 57:2)

Man's days are determined; you have decreed the number of his months and have set limits he cannot exceed.
(Job 14:5)

For God so loved the world that he gave his one and only Son, that whoever believes in him shall not perish but have eternal life.
(John 3:16)

I tell you the truth, a time is coming and has now come when the dead will hear the voice of the Son of God and those who hear will live.
(John 5:25)

I tell you the truth, if anyone keeps my word, he will never see death.
(John 8:51)

I am the resurrection and the life. He who believes in me will live, even though he dies; and whoever lives and believes in me will never die.
(John 11:25-26)

And if I go and prepare a place for you, I will come back and take you to be with me that you also may be where I am.
(John 14:3)

He is not the God of the dead, but of the living, for to him all are alive.
(Luke 20:38)

For to me, to live is Christ and to die is gain.
(Philippians 1:21)

Even though I walk through the valley of the shadow of death, I will fear no evil, for you are with me; your rod and your staff, they comfort me.
(Psalm 23:4)

But the eyes of the LORD are on those who fear him, on those whose hope is in his unfailing love, to deliver them from death and keep them alive in famine.
(Psalm 33:18-19)

But God will redeem my life from the grave; he will surely take me to himself.
(Psalm 49:15)

For you have delivered me from death and my feet from stumbling, that I may walk before God in the light of life.
(Psalm 56:13)

Our God is a God who saves; from the Sovereign LORD comes escape from death.
(Psalm 68:20)

My flesh and my heart may fail, but God is the strength of my heart and my portion forever.
(Psalm 73:26)

For you, O LORD, have delivered my soul from death, my eyes from tears, my feet from stumbling, that I may walk before the LORD in the land of the living.
(Psalm 116:8-9)

For I am convinced that neither death nor life, neither angels nor demons, neither the present nor the future, nor any powers, neither height nor depth, nor anything else in all creation, will be able to separate us from the love of God that is in Christ Jesus our Lord.
(Romans 8:38-39)

If we live, we live to the Lord; and if we die, we die to the Lord. So, whether we live or die, we belong to the Lord.
(Romans 14:8)

DENIAL

See also:
Backsliding
Darkness
Doubt
Hell
Repent
Unbelief

If anyone is ashamed of me and my words in this adulterous and sinful generation, the Son of Man will be ashamed of him when he comes in his Father's glory with the holy angels.
(Mark 8:38)

Whoever acknowledges me before men, I will also acknowledge him before my Father in heaven.
(Matthew 10:32)

But whoever disowns me before men, I will disown him before my Father in heaven.
(Matthew 10:33)

If anyone acknowledges that Jesus is the Son of God, God lives in him and he in God.
(1 John 4:15)

No one who denies the Son has the Father; whoever acknowledges the Son has the Father also.
(1 John 2:23)

Do not be afraid; keep on speaking, do not be silent. For I am with you, and no one is going to attack and harm you, because I have many people in this city.
(Acts 18:9-10)

Pray also for me, that whenever I open my mouth, words may be given me so that I will fearlessly make known the mystery of the gospel, for which I am an ambassador in chains. Pray that I may declare it fearlessly, as I should.
(Ephesians 6:19-20)

He who is not with me is against me, and he who does not gather with me, scatters.
(Luke 11:23)

And anyone who does not carry his cross and follow me cannot be my disciple.
(Luke 14:27)

Do not say, "I am only a child." You must go to everyone I send you to and say whatever I command you. Do not be afraid of them, for I am with you and will rescue you, declares the LORD.
(Jeremiah 1:7-8)

He who listens to you listens to me; he who rejects you rejects me; but he who rejects me rejects him who sent me.
(Luke 10:16)

I speak of your faithfulness and salvation. I do not conceal your love and your truth from the great assembly.
(Psalm 40:10)

Through Jesus, therefore, let us continually offer to God a sacrifice of praise — the fruit of lips that confess his name.
(Hebrews 13:15)

I eagerly expect and hope that I will in no way be ashamed, but will have sufficient courage so that now as always Christ will be exalted in my body, whether by life or by death.
(Philippians 1:20)

DEPRESSION, SYMPTOMS OF

See also:
Anxiety/Worry
Darkness
Dissatisfaction
Grief
Guilt/Shame
Help
Hopeless
Self-Esteem, Low
Sleep Problems
Sorrow
Strength
Thinking, Unhealthy
Tired
Weakness

Why are you downcast, O my soul? Why so distrubed within me? Put your hope in God.
(Psalm 43:5)

Find rest, O my soul, in God alone; my hope comes from him.
(Psalm 62:5)

Anyone who is among the living has hope.
(Ecclesiastes 9:4)

Everything is possible for him who believes.
(Mark 9:23)

The LORD is close to the brokenhearted and saves those who are crushed in spirit.
(Psalm 34:18)

Surely he took up our infirmities and carried our sorrows.
(Isaiah 53:4)

He heals the brokenhearted and binds up their wounds.
(Psalm 147:3)

The LORD upholds all those who fall and lifts up all who are bowed down.
(Psalm 145:14)

The Lord knows how to rescue godly men from trials.
(2 Peter 2:9)

Be strong in the LORD and in his mighty power.
(Ephesians 6:10)

Look to the LORD and his strength; seek his face always.
(Psalm 105:4)

My help comes from the LORD, the Maker of heaven and earth.
(Psalm 121:2)

God is our refuge and strength, an ever-present help in
trouble.
(Psalm 46:1)

God is light; in him there is no darkness at all.
(1 John 1:5)

You, O LORD, keep my light burning; my God turns my
darkness into light.
(Psalm 18:28)

The LORD is near. Do not be anxious about anything.
(Philippians 4:5)

The LORD is near to all who call on him, to all who call on
him in truth.
(Psalm 145:18)

Come near to God and he will come near to you.
(James 4:8)

When I was in great need, he saved me.
(Psalm 116:6)

The Sovereign LORD will wipe away the tears from all faces.
(Isaiah 25:8)

He will lead them to springs of living water. And God
will wipe away every tear from their eyes.
(Revelation 7:17)

DEVIL

See also:
Antichrist
End Times
Evil, Resisting
Lord's Prayer
Occult
Temptation

*And lead us not into temptation, but
deliver us from the evil one.*
(Matt 6:13)

*My prayer is not that you take them out
of the world but that you protect them from the evil one.*
(John 17:15)

For our struggle is not against flesh and blood, but
against the rulers, against the authorities, against the
powers of this dark world and against the spiritual forces
of evil in the heavenly realms.
(Ephesians 6:12)

Resist the devil, and he will flee from you.
(James 4:7)

Put on the full armor of God so that you can take your
stand against the devil's schemes.
(Ephesians 6:11)

Be self-controlled and alert. Your enemy the devil prowls
around like a roaring lion looking for someone to devour.
Resist him, standing firm in the faith, because you know
that your brothers throughout the world are undergoing
the same kind of sufferings.
(1 Peter 5:8-9)

He who does what is sinful is of the devil, because the
devil has been sinning from the beginning.
(1 John 3:8)

This is how we know who the children of God are and who the children of the devil are: Anyone who does not do what is right is not a child of God; nor is anyone who does not love his brother.
(1 John 3:10)

We know that we are children of God, and that the whole world is under the control of the evil one.
(1 John 5:19)

Satan himself masquerades as an angel of light.
(2 Corinthians 11:14)

When he lies, he speaks his native language, for he is a liar and the father of lies.
(John 8:44)

He was a murderer from the beginning, not holding to the truth, for there is no truth in him.
(John 8:44)

But the Lord is faithful, and he will strengthen and protect you from the evil one.
(2 Thessalonians 3:3)

The reason the Son of God appeared was to destroy the devil's work.
(1 John 3:8)

The one who is in you is greater than the one who is in the world.
(1 John 4:4)

The God of peace will soon crush Satan under your feet.
(Romans 16:20)

Now is the time for judgment on this world; now the prince of this world will be driven out.
(John 12:31)

And the devil, who deceived them, was thrown into the lake of burning sulfur, where the beast and the false prophet had been thrown. They will be tormented day and night for ever and ever.
(Revelation 20:10)

DISASTER

See also:
Death/Dying
Grief
Hardship
Help
Hopeless
Protection
Refuge/Safety
Sickness
Strength
Suffering
Troubles
Weakness

Have no fear of sudden disaster or of the ruin that overtakes the wicked, for the LORD will be your confidence and will keep your foot from being snared.
(Proverbs 3:25)

I will take refuge in the shadow of your wings until the disaster has passed.
(Psalm 57:1)

In God I trust; I will not be afraid.
(Psalm 56:4)

If the earthly tent we live in is destroyed, we have a building from God, an eternal house in heaven, not built by human hands.
(2 Corinthians 5:1)

When calamity comes, the wicked are brought down, but even in death the righteous have a refuge.
(Proverbs 14:32)

Then you will call, and the LORD will answer; you will cry for help, and he will say: Here am I.
(Isaiah 58:9)

I call on the LORD in my distress, and he answers me.
(Psalm 120:1)

For he has delivered me from all my troubles.
(Psalm 54:7)

He brought me out into a spacious place; he rescued me
because he delighted in me.
(Psalm 18:19)

Though I walk in the midst of trouble, you preserve my
life; you stretch out your hand against the anger of my
foes, with your right hand you save me.
(Psalm 138:7)

For your name's sake, O LORD, preserve my life; in your
righteousness, bring me out of trouble.
(Psalm 143:11)

In this you greatly rejoice, though now for a little while
you may have had to suffer grief in all kinds of trials.
These have come so that your faith--of greater worth than
gold, which perishes even though refined by fire--may be
proved genuine and may result in praise, glory and
honor when Jesus Christ is revealed.
(1 Peter 1:6-7)

The LORD will keep you from all harm--he will watch
over your life; the LORD will watch over your coming and
going both now and forevermore.
(Psalm 121:7-8)

DISCIPLINE

See also:
Rebuke/Correction

Whoever loves discipline loves knowledge, but he who hates correction is stupid.
(Proverbs 12:1)

He will die for lack of discipline, led astray by his own
great folly.
(Proverbs 5:23)

No discipline seems pleasant at the time, but painful.
Later on, however, it produces a harvest of righteousness
and peace for those who have been trained by it.
(Hebrews 12:11)

He who heeds discipline shows the way to life, but whoever ignores correction leads others astray.
(Proverbs 10:17)

He who ignores discipline comes to poverty and shame,
but whoever heeds correction is honored.
(Proverbs 13:18)

If you are not disciplined (and everyone undergoes discipline), then you are illegitimate children and not true sons.
(Hebrews 12:8)

We have all had human fathers who disciplined us and
we respected them for it. How much more should we
submit to the Father of our spirits and live!
(Hebrews 12:9)

Our fathers disciplined us for a little while as they
thought best; but God disciplines for our good, that we
may share in his holiness.
(Hebrews 12:10)

Blessed is the man whom God corrects; so do not despise the discipline of the Almighty. For he wounds, but he also binds up; he injures, but his hands also heal.
(Job 5:17-18)

The corrections of discipline are the way to life, keeping you from the immoral woman, from the smooth tongue of the wayward wife.
(Proverbs 6:23-24)

You rebuke and discipline men for their sin.
(Psalm 39:11)

Blows and wounds cleanse away evil, and beatings purge the inmost being.
(Proverbs 20:30)

The LORD has chastened me severely, but he has not given me over to death.
(Psalm 118:18)

Blessed is the man you discipline, O LORD, the man you teach from your law.
(Psalm 94:12)

DISHONESTY

See also:
Lying
Slander
Ten Commandments

Do not steal.
(Leviticus 19:11)

Whoever is dishonest with very little will also be dishonest with much.
(Luke 16:10)

Do not trust in extortion or take pride in stolen goods.
(Psalm 62:10)

Ill-gotten treasures are of no value, but righteousness delivers from death.
(Proverbs 10:2)

The wicked man earns deceptive wages, but he who sows righteousness reaps a sure reward.
(Proverbs 11:18)

A fortune made by a lying tongue is a fleeting vapor and a deadly snare.
(Proverbs 21:6)

Extortion turns a wise man into a fool, and a bribe corrupts the heart.
(Ecclesiastes 7:7)

Food gained by fraud tastes sweet to a man, but he ends up with a mouthful of gravel.
(Proverbs 20:17)

The LORD abhors dishonest scales, but accurate weights are his delight.
(Proverbs 11:1)

The way of the guilty is devious, but the conduct of the innocent is upright.
(Proverbs 21:8)

He whose walk is upright fears the LORD, but he whose ways are devious despises him.
(Proverbs 14:2)

The righteous detest the dishonest; the wicked detest the upright.
(Proverbs 29:27)

The man of integrity walks securely, but he who takes crooked paths will be found out.
(Proverbs 10:9)

The scoundrel's methods are wicked, he makes up evil schemes to destroy the poor with lies, even when the plea of the needy is just.
(Isaiah 32:7)

Like a partridge that hatches eggs it did not lay is the man who gains riches by unjust means. When his life is half gone, they will desert him, and in the end he will prove to be a fool.
(Jeremiah 17:11)

He who has been stealing must steal no longer, but must work, doing something useful with his own hands, that he may have something to share with those in need.
(Ephesians 4:28)

So if you have not been trustworthy in handling worldly wealth, who will trust you with true riches?
(Luke 16:11)

DISOBEDIENCE

See also:
Backsliding
Darkness
Evil, Resisting
Obedience
Sin, Consequences Of

Why do you call me, 'Lord, Lord,'
and do not do what I say?
(Luke 6:46)

You were running a good race. Who cut in on you and
kept you from obeying the truth?
(Galatians 5:7)

See how each of you is following the stubbornness of his
evil heart instead of obeying me.
(Jeremiah 16:12)

I look on the faithless with loathing, for they do not obey
your word.
(Psalm 119:158)

Streams of tears flow from my eyes, for your law is not
obeyed.
(Psalm 119:136)

Anyone who runs ahead and does not continue in the
teaching of Christ does not have God; whoever continues
in the teaching has both the Father and the Son.
(2 John 1:9)

The man who says, "I know him," but does not do what
he commands is a liar, and the truth is not in him.
(1 John 2:4)

But if anyone obeys his word, God's love is truly made
complete in him.
(1 John 2:5)

He who obeys instructions guards his life, but he who is contemptuous of his ways will die.
(Proverbs 19:16)

We must obey God rather than men!
(Acts 5:29)

Walk in all the ways I command you, that it may go well with you.
(Jeremiah 7:23)

If you fear the LORD and serve and obey him and do not rebel against his commands, and if both you and the king who reigns over you follow the LORD your God — good!
(1 Samuel 12:14)

Oh, that their hearts would be inclined to fear me and keep all my commands always, so that it might go well with them and their children forever!
(Deuteronomy 5:29)

Remember, therefore, what you have received and heard; obey it, and repent.
(Revelation 3:3)

DISSATISFACTION

See also:
Christ, Identity Of
Communion
Eternal Life
Gifts, Physical/
   Material
Truth

You open your hand and satisfy the
desire of every living thing.
(Psalm 145:16)

His divine power has given us everything we need for
life and godliness through our knowledge of him who
called us by his own glory and goodness.
(2 Peter 1:3)

*For the bread of God is he who comes down from heaven and
gives life to the world.*
(John 6:33)

*I am the bread of life. He who comes to me will never go hun-
gry, and he who believes in me will never be thirsty.*
(John 6:35)

If anyone is thirsty, let him come to me and drink.
(John 7:38)

*Whoever believes in me, as the Scripture has said, streams of
living water will flow from within him.*
(John 7:38)

*Everyone who drinks of this water will be thirsty again, but
whoever drinks the water I give him will never thirst.*
(John 4:13-14)

*Indeed, the water I give him will become in him a spring of
water welling up to eternal life.*
(John 4:14)

O God, you are my God, earnestly I seek you; my soul thirsts for you, my body longs for you, in a dry and weary land where there is no water.
(Psalm 63:1)

My soul thirsts for God, for the living God. When can I go and meet with God?
(Psalm 42:2)

He will lead them to springs of living water. And God will wipe away every tear from their eyes.
(Revelation 7:17)

Blessed are you who hunger now, for you will be satisfied.
(Luke 6:21)

My soul will be satisfied as with the richest of foods; with singing lips my mouth will praise you.
(Psalm 63:5)

For he satisfies the thirsty and fills the hungry with good things.
(Psalm 107:9)

"Come!" Whoever is thirsty, let him come; and whoever wishes, let him take the free gift of the water of life.
(Revelation 22:17)

Satisfy us in the morning with your unfailing love, that we may sing for joy and be glad all our days.
(Psalm 90:14)

DIVORCE

"I hate divorce," says the LORD
God of Israel.
(Malachi 2:16)

See also:
Adultery
Lust
Marriage
Marriage Guidance
Promiscuity

*Moses permitted you to divorce your wives because your hearts
were hard. But it was not this way from the beginning.*
(Matthew 19:8)

*It has been said, "Anyone who divorces his wife must give her
a certificate of divorce." But I tell you that anyone who divorces his wife, except for marital unfaithfulness, causes her to
become an adulteress, and anyone who marries the divorced
woman commits adultery.*
(Matthew 5:31-32)

Therefore what God has joined together, let man not separate.
(Mark 10:9)

*I tell you that anyone who divorces his wife, except for marital
unfaithfulness, and marries another woman commits adultery.*
(Matthew 19:9)

*And if she divorces her husband and marries another man, she
commits adultery.*
(Mark 10:12)

To the married I give this command (not I, but the Lord):
A wife must not separate from her husband. But if she
does, she must remain unmarried or else be reconciled to
her husband. And a husband must not divorce his wife.
(1 Corinthians 7:10-11)

Anyone who divorces his wife and marries another woman commits adultery, and the man who marries a divorced woman commits adultery.
(Luke 16:18)

Like a bird that strays from its nest is a man who strays from his home.
(Proverbs 27:8)

If a man divorces his wife and she leaves him and marries another man, should he return to her again? Would not the land be completely defiled?
(Jeremiah 3:1)

If any brother has a wife who is not a believer and she is willing to live with him, he must not divorce her.
(1 Corinthians 7:12)

And if a woman has a husband who is not a believer and he is willing to live with her, she must not divorce him.
(1 Corinthians 7:13)

But if the unbeliever leaves, let him do so. A believing man or woman is not bound in such circumstances; God has called us to live in peace.
(1 Corinthians 7:15)

If anyone does not provide for his relatives, and especially for his immediate family, he has denied the faith and is worse than an unbeliever.
(1 Timothy 5:8)

He who brings trouble on his family will inherit only wind, and the fool will be servant to the wise.
(Proverbs 11:29)

DOUBT

See also:
Backsliding
Darkness
Denial
Faith
Temptation
Unbelief

Stop doubting and believe.
(John 20:27)

*Put your finger here; see my hands. Reach
out your hand and put it into my side.*
(John 20:27)

Be on your guard; stand firm in the faith; be men of courage;
be strong.
(1 Corinthians 16:13)

Remain in me, and I will remain in you.
(John 15:4)

If we are faithless, he will remain faithful, for he cannot
disown himself.
(2 Timothy 2:13)

Now it is God who makes both us and you stand firm in
Christ. He anointed us, set his seal of ownership on us, and
put his Spirit in our hearts as a deposit, guaranteeing what is
to come.
(2 Corinthians 1:21-22)

The disciples went and woke him, saying, "Master, Master,
we're going to drown!" He got up and rebuked the wind
and the raging waters; the storm subsided, and all was calm.
Where is your faith? he asked his disciples.
(Luke 8:24-25)

*If you have faith as small as a mustard seed, you can say to this
mulberry tree, "Be uprooted and planted in the sea," and it will
obey you.*
(Luke 17:6)

Have faith in God, Jesus answered. *I tell you the truth, if anyone says to this mountain, "Go, throw yourself into the sea," and does not doubt in his heart but believes that what he says will happen, it will be done for him.*
(Mark 11:22-23)

I tell you the truth, if you have faith and do not doubt, not only can you do what was done to the fig tree, but also you can say to this mountain, "Go, throw yourself into the sea," and it will be done.
(Matthew 21:21)

See that what you have heard from the beginning remains in you. If it does, you also will remain in the Son and in the Father.
(1 John 2:24)

And now, dear children, continue in him, so that when he appears we may be confident and unashamed before him at his coming.
(1 John 2:28)

DRUG ABUSE

See also:
Alcoholism
Anger
Backsliding
Guilt/Shame
Hopeless
Repent
Self-Esteem, Low
Strength
Temptation
Weakness

Don't you know that you yourselves are God's temple and that
God's Spirit lives in you? If anyone
destroys God's temple, God will
destroy him; for God's temple is
sacred, and you are that temple.
(1 Corinthians 3:16-17)

For we are the temple of the living God.
(2 Corinthians 6:16)

Let us purify ourselves from everything that contami-
nates body and spirit, perfecting holiness out of reverence for God.
(2 Corinthians 7:1)

A man is a slave to whatever has mastered him.
(2 Peter 2:19)

So I say, live by the Spirit, and you will not gratify the
desires of a sinful nature. For the sinful nature desires
what is contrary to the Spirit, and the Spirit what is
contrary to the sinful nature.
(Galatians 5:16-17)

*I tell you the truth, everyone who sins is a slave to sin. Now a
slave has no permanent place in the family, but a son belongs
to it forever.*
(John 8:34-35)

For I have the desire to do what is good, but I cannot
carry it out.
(Romans 7:18)

For what I do is not the good I want to do; no, the evil I do not want to do — this I keep doing.
(Romans 7:19)

What a wretched man I am! Who will rescue me from this body of death? Thanks be to God — through Jesus Christ our Lord!
(Romans 7:24-25)

Those controlled by the sinful nature cannot please God.
(Romans 8:8)

You, however, are controlled not by the sinful nature but by the Spirit, if the Spirit of God lives in you.
(Romans 8:9)

For if you live according to the sinful nature, you will die; but if by the Spirit you put to death the misdeeds of the body, you will live, because those who are led by the Spirit of God are sons of God.
(Romans 8:13-14)

Clothe yourselves with the Lord Jesus Christ, and do not think about how to gratify the desires of the sinful nature.
(Romans 13:14)

ELDERLY

See also:
Eternal Life
God, Eternal
Heaven
Sickness
Sleep Problems
Strength
Suffering
Weakness
Wisdom

Rise in the presence of the aged, show respect for the elderly and revere your God. I am the LORD.
(Leviticus 19:32)

Is not wisdom found among the aged? Does not long life bring understanding?
(Job 12:12)

Gray hair is a crown of splendor; it is attained by a righteous life.
(Proverbs 16:31)

The glory of young men is their strength, gray hair the splendor of the old.
(Proverbs 20:29)

Children's children are a crown to the aged.
(Proverbs 17:6)

Teach the older men to be temperate, worthy of respect, self-controlled, and sound in faith, in love and in endurance.
(Titus 2:2)

Likewise, teach the older women to be reverent in the way they live, not to be slanderers or addicted to much wine, but to teach what is good.
(Titus 2:3)

Then they can train the younger women to love their husbands and children, to be self-controlled and pure, to be busy at home, to be kind, and to be subject to their husbands, so that no one will malign the word of God.
(Titus 2:4-5)

Do not cast me away when I am old; do not forsake me when my strength is gone.
(Psalm 71:9)

Even when I am old and gray, do not forsake me, O God, till I declare your power to the next generation, your might to all who are to come.
(Psalm 71:18)

END TIMES

The end of all things is near.
Therefore be clear minded and
self-controlled so that you can pray.
(1 Peter 4:7)

In the last days, God says, I will pour
out my spirit on all people. Your sons
and daughters will prophesy, your
young men will see visions, your old
men will dream dreams.
(Acts 2:17)

*I tell you, on that night two people will be in one bed; one will
be taken and the other left.*
(Luke 17:34)

*For many will come in my name, claiming, "I am he," and,
"The time is near." Do not follow them.*
(Luke 21:8)

*When you hear of wars and revolutions, do not be frightened. These
things must happen first, but the end will not come right away.*
(Luke 21:9)

Nation will rise against nation, and kingdom against kingdom.
(Luke 21:10)

*There will be great earthquakes, famines and pestilences in
various places, and fearful events and great signs from heaven.*
(Luke 21:11)

But before all this, they will lay hands on you and persecute you. They will deliver you to synagogues and prisons, and you will be brought before kings and governors, and all on account of my name.
(Luke 21:12)

You will be betrayed even by parents, brothers, relatives and friends, and they will put some of you to death.
(Luke 21:16)

But not a hair on your head will perish.
(Luke 21:18)

By standing firm you will gain life.
(Luke 21:19)

When you see Jerusalem being surrounded by armies, you will know that its desolation is near.
(Luke 21:20)

Jerusalem will be trampled on by the Gentiles until the times of the Gentiles are fulfilled.
(Luke 21:24)

On the earth, nations will be in anguish and perplexity at the roaring and tossing of the sea.
(Luke 21:25)

There will be signs in the sun, moon and stars.
(Luke 21:25)

Men will faint from terror, apprehensive of what is coming on the world, for the heavenly bodies will be shaken.
(Luke 21:26)

When these things begin to take place, stand up and lift up your heads, because your redemption is drawing near.
(Luke 21:28)

When you see these things happening, you know that the kingdom of God is near.
(Luke 21:31)

I tell you the truth, some who are standing here will not taste death before they see the kingdom of God come with power.
(Mark 9:1)

No one knows about that day or hour, not even the angels in heaven, nor the Son, but only the Father.
(Matthew 24:36)

ENVY/JEALOUSY

A heart at peace gives life to the
body, but envy rots the bones.
(Proverbs 14:30)

See also:
Greedy/Stingy
Money
Poverty
Riches, Beware Of
Riches, True
Worldly

You shall not set your desire on your
neighbor's house or land, his manservant or maidservant,
his ox or donkey, or anything that belongs to your neighbor.
(Deuteronomy 5:21)

And I saw that all labor and all achievement spring from
man's envy of his neighbor. This too is meaningless, a
chasing after the wind.
(Ecclesiastes 4:4)

Let us not become conceited, provoking and envying
each other.
(Galatians 5:26)

If you harbor bitter envy and selfish ambition in your
hearts, do not boast about it or deny the truth. Such
"wisdom" does not come down from heaven but is
earthly, unspiritual, of the devil.
(James 3:14-15)

For where you have envy and selfish ambition, there you
find disorder and every evil practice.
(James 3:16)

Therefore, rid yourselves of all malice and all deceit,
hypocrisy, envy, and slander of every kind.
(1 Peter 2:1)

Do not let your heart envy sinners, but always be zealous
for the fear of the LORD.
(Proverbs 23:17)

Do not fret because of evil men or be envious of those
who do wrong; for like the grass they will soon wither,
like green plants they will soon die away.
(Psalm 37:1-2)

Do not fret when men succeed in their ways, when they
carry out their wicked schemes.
(Psalm 37:7)

For I envied the arrogant when I saw the prosperity of
the wicked.
(Psalm 73:3)

Do not be overawed when a man grows rich, when the
splendor of his house increases; for he will take nothing
with him when he dies, his splendor will not descend
with him.
(Psalm 49:16-17)

ETERNAL LIFE

See also:
Born Again
Christ, Mission Of
Confession
Heaven
Salvation

God has given us eternal life, and this life is in his Son.
(1 John 5:11)

I tell you the truth, whoever hears my word and believes him who sent me has eternal life and will not be condemned; he has crossed over from death to life.
(John 5:24)

Now this is eternal life: that they may know you, the only true God, and Jesus Christ, whom you have sent.
(John 17:3)

I give them eternal life, and they shall never perish; no one can snatch them out of my hand.
(John 10:28)

My Father, who has given them to me, is greater than all; no one can snatch them out of my Father's hand.
(John 10:29)

So we fix our eyes not on what is seen, but on what is unseen. For what is seen is temporary, but what is unseen is eternal.
(2 Corinthians 4:18)

The man who loves his life will lose it, while the man who hates his life in this world will keep it for eternal life.
(John 12:25)

He has made everything beautiful in its time. He has also set eternity in the hearts of men; yet they cannot fathom what God has done from beginning to end.
(Ecclesiastes 3:11)

For the trumpet will sound, the dead will be raised imperishable, and we will be changed. For the perishable must clothe itself with the imperishable, and the mortal with immortality.
(1 Corinthians 15:52-53)

My sheep listen to my voice; I know them, and they follow me. I give them eternal life, and they shall never perish; no one can snatch them out of my hand. My Father, who has given them to me, is greater than all; no one can snatch them out of my Father's hand.
(John 10:27-29)

In the way of righteousness there is life; along that path is immortality.
(Proverbs 12:28)

To those who by persistence in doing good seek glory, honor and immortality, he will give eternal life.
(Romans 2:7)

EVIL, RESISTING

See also:
Antichrist
Backsliding
Devil
End Times
Occult
Temptation
Truth

Dear children, do not let anyone lead
you astray.
(1 John 3:7)

As obedient children, do not conform to
the evil desires you had when you lived
in ignorance.
(1 Peter 1:14)

But just as he who called you is holy, so be holy in all you
do; for it is written: "Be holy, because I am holy."
(1 Peter 1:15-16)

Test everything. Hold on to the good. Avoid every kind
of evil.
(1 Thessalonians 5:21-22)

Everyone who confesses the name of the Lord must turn
away from wickedness.
(2 Timothy 2:19)

The fear of the Lord — that is wisdom, and to shun evil is
understanding.
(Job 28:28)

Through the fear of the LORD a man avoids evil.
(Proverbs 16:6)

Be on your guard so that you may not be carried away by
the error of lawless men and fall from your secure position.
(2 Peter 3:17)

In the paths of the wicked lie thorns and snares, but he who guards his soul stays far from them.
(Proverbs 22:5)

Turn from evil and do good; then you will dwell in the land forever.
(Psalm 37:27)

Dear friend, do not imitate what is evil but what is good. Anyone who does what is good is from God. Anyone who does what is evil has not seen God.
(3 John 1:11)

Woe to those who call evil good and good evil, who put darkness for light and light for darkness, who put bitter for sweet and sweet for bitter.
(Isaiah 5:20)

This is what the LORD says: "Maintain justice and do what is right, for my salvation is close at hand and my righteousness will soon be revealed."
(Isaiah 56:1)

Everyone who does evil hates the light, and will not come into the light for fear that his deeds will be exposed.
(John 3:20)

Your eye is the lamp of your body. When your eyes are good, your whole body also is full of light. But when they are bad, your body also is full of darkness. See to it then, that the light within you is not darkness.
(Luke 11:34-35)

Deliver me, O my God, from the hand of the wicked, from the grasp of evil and cruel men.
(Psalm 71:4)

Let not my heart be drawn to what is evil, to take part in wicked deeds with men who are evildoers; let me not eat of their delicacies.
(Psalm 141:4)

Keep me from the snares they have laid for me, from the traps set by evildoers.
(Psalm 141:9)

Hate what is evil; cling to what is good.
(Romans 12:9)

Do not be overcome by evil, but overcome evil with good.
(Romans 12:21)

FAITH

See also:
Belief
Born Again
Repent
Salvation

Now faith is being sure of what we
hope for and certain of what we do
not see.
(Hebrews 11:1)

We live by faith, not by sight.
(2 Corinthians 5:7)

Faith comes from hearing the message, and the message
is heard through the word of Christ.
(Romans 10:17)

Build yourselves up in your most holy faith and pray in
the Holy Spirit.
(Jude 1:20)

By faith we eagerly await through the Spirit the
righteousness for which we hope.
(Galatians 5:5)

Fight the good fight of the faith.
(1 Timothy 6:12)

Examine yourselves to see whether you are in the faith;
test yourselves. Do you not realize that Christ Jesus is in
you — unless, of course, you fail the test?
(2 Corinthians 13:5)

Everything that does not come from faith is sin.
(Romans 14:23)

Now it is required that those who have been given a trust
must prove faithful.
(1 Corinthians 4:2)

For this very reason, make every effort to add to your faith goodness; and to goodness, knowledge; and to knowledge, self-control; and to self-control, perseverance; and to perseverance, godliness; and to godliness, brotherly kindness; and to brotherly kindness, love.
(2 Peter 1:5-7)

Let us fix our eyes on Jesus, the author and perfecter of our faith.
(Hebrews 12:2)

Righteousness will be his belt and faithfulness the sash around his waist.
(Isaiah 11:5)

The LORD preserves the faithful, but the proud he pays back in full.
(Psalm 31:23)

For the LORD loves the just and will not forsake his faithful ones.
(Psalm 37:28)

My heart is steadfast, O God, my heart is steadfast; I will sing and make music.
(Psalm 57:7)

I have fought the good fight, I have finished the race, I have kept the faith.
(2 Timothy 4:7)

Be faithful, even to the point of death, and I will give you the crown of life.
(Revelation 2:10)

FEAR

See also:
Anxiety/Worry
Psalm 23

The LORD is my light and my salvation — whom shall I fear? The LORD is the stronghold of my life — of whom shall I be afraid?
(Psalm 27:1)

Even though I walk through the valley of the shadow of death, I will fear no evil, for you are with me; your rod and your staff, they comfort me.
(Psalm 23:4)

Do not be afraid, little flock, for your Father has been pleased to give you the kingdom.
(Luke 12:32)

When I am afraid, I will trust in you.
(Psalm 56:3)

The LORD watches over all who love him.
(Psalm 145:20)

There is no fear in love. But perfect love drives out fear, because fear has to do with punishment. The one who fears is not made perfect in love.
(1 John 4:18)

You of little faith, why are you so afraid?
(Matthew 8:26)

Don't be afraid; just believe.
(Mark 5:36)

Stand firm in one spirit, contending as one man for the faith of the gospel, without being frightened in any way by those who oppose you.
(Philippians 1:27-28)

For you did not receive a spirit that makes you a slave again to fear, but you received the Spirit of sonship.
(Romans 8:15)

The Lord is my helper; I will not be afraid.
(Hebrews 13:6)

The LORD is with me; I will not be afraid. What can man do to me?
(Psalm 118:6)

Fear of man will prove to be a snare, but whoever trusts in the Lord is kept safe.
(Proverbs 29:25)

I tell you, my friends, do not be afraid of those who kill the body and after that can do no more. But I will show you whom you should fear: Fear him who, after the killing of the body, has the power to throw you into hell. Yes, I tell you, fear him.
(Luke 12:4-5)

The fear of the LORD is the beginning of knowledge.
(Proverbs 1:7)

Do not be afraid of those who kill the body but cannot kill the soul. Rather, be afraid of the One who can destroy both soul and body in hell.
(Matthew 10:28)

Strengthen the feeble hands, steady the knees that give way; say to those with fearful hearts, "Be strong, do not fear; your God will come."
(Isaiah 35:3-4)

I sought the LORD, and he answered me; he delivered me from all my fears.
(Psalm 34:4)

Therefore we will not fear, though the earth give way and the mountains fall into the heart of the sea, though its waters roar and foam and the mountains quake with their surging.
(Psalm 46:2-3)

Surely God is my salvation; I will trust and not be afraid.
(Isaiah 12:2)

FORGIVE

See also:
Anger
Forgiveness
Hatred
Judgmental
Lord's Prayer
Love, For Others
Vengeance

Forgive, and you will be forgiven.
(Luke 6:37)

If he sins against you seven times in a day, and seven times comes back to you and says, "I repent," forgive him.
(Luke 17:4)

And when you stand praying, if you hold anything against anyone, forgive him, so that your Father in heaven may forgive you your sins.
(Mark 11:25)

Forgive us our debts, as we also have forgiven our debtors.
(Matthew 6:12)

For if you forgive men when they sin against you, your heavenly Father will also forgive you. But if you do not forgive men their sins, your Father will not forgive your sins.
(Matthew 6:14-15)

Be kind and compassionate to one another, forgiving each other, just as in Christ God forgave you.
(Ephesians 4:32)

Bear with each other and forgive whatever grievances you may have against one another. Forgive as the Lord forgave you.
(Colossians 3:13)

Then Peter came to Jesus and asked, "Lord, how many times shall I forgive my brother when he sins against me? Up to seven times?" Jesus answered, *I tell you, not seven times, but seventy-seven times.*
(Matthew 18:21-22)

FORGIVENESS

See also:
Blasphemy
Christ, Mission Of
Confession
Forgive

God demonstrates his own love for us in this: While we were still sinners, Christ died for us.
(Romans 5:8)

For he bore the sin of many, and made intercession for the transgressors.
(Isaiah 53:12)

God was reconciling the world to himself in Christ, not counting men's sins against them.
(2 Corinthians 5:19)

For God did not send his Son into the world to condemn the world, but to save the world through him. Whoever believes in him is not condemned.
(John 3:17-18)

Therefore, there is now no condemnation for those who are in Christ Jesus, because through Christ Jesus the law of the Spirit of life set me free from the law of sin and death.
(Romans 8:1-2)

Everyone who believes in him receives forgiveness of sins through his name.
(Acts 10:43)

The LORD redeems his servants; no one will be condemned who takes refuge in him.
(Psalm 34:22)

I did not come to judge the world but to save it.
(John 12:47)

So if the Son sets you free, you will be free indeed.
(John 8:36)

In your love you kept me from the pit of destruction; you have put all my sins behind your back.
(Isaiah 38:17)

You forgave the iniquity of your people and covered all their sins.
(Psalm 85:2)

Blessed is the man whose sin the Lord will never count against him.
(Romans 4:8)

Their sins and lawless acts I will remember no more.
(Hebrews 10:17)

As far as the east is from the west, so far has he removed our transgressions from us.
(Psalm 103:12)

For we know that our old self was crucified with him so that the body of sin might be done away with, that we should no longer be slaves to sin — because anyone who has died has been freed from sin.
(Romans 6:6-7)

May your whole spirit, soul and body be kept blameless at the coming of our Lord Jesus Christ.
(1 Thessalonians 5:23)

FRIENDSHIP

See also:
Church
Impatient
Love, For Others

Each of you should look not only to
your own interests, but also to the
interests of others.
(Philippians 2:4)

Speak to one another with psalms, hymns and spiritual
songs.
(Ephesians 5:19)

Submit to one another out of reverence for Christ.
(Ephesians 5:21)

Do not forget to entertain strangers, for by so doing some
people have entertained angels without knowing it.
(Hebrews 13:2)

A righteous man is cautious in friendship, but the way of
the wicked leads them astray.
(Proverbs 12:26)

I do not sit with deceitful men, nor do I consort with hypocrites; I abhor the assembly of evil doers and refuse to sit
with the wicked.
(Psalm 26:4-5)

A man of many companions may come to ruin, but there
is a friend who sticks closer than a brother.
(Proverbs 18:24)

As iron sharpens iron, so one man sharpens another.
(Proverbs 27:17)

Two are better than one, because they have a good return for their work: If one falls down, his friend can help him up!
(Ecclesiastes 4:9-10)

A friend loves at all times, and a brother is born for adversity.
(Proverbs 17:17)

Perfume and incense bring joy to the heart, and the pleasantness of one's friend springs from his earnest counsel.
(Proverbs 27:9)

Seldom set foot in your neighbor's house — too much of you, and he will hate you.
(Proverbs 25:17)

Do not forsake your friend and the friend of your father, and do not go to your brother's house when disaster strikes you — better a neighbor nearby than a brother far away.
(Proverbs 27:10)

How good and pleasant it is when brothers live together in unity!
(Psalm 133:1)

FRUITFUL

See also:
Action
Witness

The fruit of the righteous is a tree of life,
and he who wins souls is wise.
(Proverbs 11:30)

*No branch can bear fruit by itself; it must remain in the vine.
Neither can you bear fruit unless you remain in me.*
(John 15:4)

*I am the vine; you are the branches. If a man remains in me
and I in him, he will bear much fruit; apart from me you can do
nothing.*
(John 15:5)

*If anyone does not remain in me, he is like a branch that is
thrown away and withers; such branches are picked up, thrown
into the fire and burned.*
(John 15:6)

*This is to my Father's glory, that you bear much fruit, showing
yourselves to be my disciples.*
(John 15:8)

*You did not choose me, but I chose you and appointed you to go
and bear fruit — fruit that will last. Then the father will give
you whatever you ask in my name.*
(John 15:16)

*No good tree bears bad fruit, nor does a bad tree bear good
fruit. Each tree is recognized by its own fruit.*
(Luke 6:43-44)

*Every tree that does not bear good fruit is cut down and
thrown into the fire. Thus, by their fruit you will recognize
them.*
(Matthew 7:19)

The harvest is plentiful but the workers are few.
(Matthew 9:37)

The man who plants and the man who waters have one purpose, and each will be rewarded according to his own labor. For we are God's fellow workers; you are God's field, God's building.
(1 Corinthians 3:8-9)

Remember this: Whoever sows sparingly will also reap sparingly, and whoever sows generously will also reap generously.
(2 Corinthians 9:6)

Whoever turns a sinner from the error of his way will save him from death and cover a multitude of sins.
(James 5:20)

But thanks be to God, who always leads us in triumphal procession in Christ and through us spreads everywhere the fragrance of the knowledge of him.
(2 Corinthians 2:14)

GIFTS, PHYSICAL/ MATERIAL

See also:
Poverty
Riches, Beware Of
Riches, True

The LORD bestows favor and honor; no good thing does he withhold from those whose walk is blameless.
(Psalm 84:11)

Every good and perfect gift is from above, coming down from the Father of the heavenly lights, who does not change like shifting shadows.
(James 1:17)

Now the Lord is the Spirit, and where the Spirit of the Lord is, there is freedom.
(2 Corinthians 3:17)

That everyone may eat and drink, and find satisfaction in all his toil—this is the gift of God.
(Ecclesiastes 3:13)

For everything God created is good, and nothing is to be rejected if it is received with thanksgiving, because it is consecrated by the word of God and prayer.
(1 Timothy 4:4-5)

Moreover, when God gives any man wealth and possessions, and enables him to enjoy them, to accept his lot and be happy in his work—this is a gift of God. He seldom reflects on the days of his life, because God keeps him occupied with gladness of heart.
(Ecclesiastes 5:19-20)

The lions may grow weak and hungry, but those who seek the LORD lack no good thing.
(Psalm 34:10)

You have granted him the desire of his heart and have not withheld the request of his lips.
(Psalm 21:2)

He who did not spare his own Son, but gave him up for us all—how will he not also, along with him, graciously give us all things?
(Romans 8:32)

GIFTS, SPIRITUAL

See also:
Church
Holy Spirit
Holy Spirit, Pentecost

Each man has his own gift from God; one has this gift, another has that.
(1 Corinthians 7:7)

There are different kinds of gifts, but the same Spirit.
(1 Corinthians 12:4)

We have different gifts, according to the grace given us.
(Romans 12:6)

Now to each one the manifestation of the Spirit is given for the common good. To one there is given through the Spirit the message of wisdom, to another the message of knowledge by means of the same Spirit, to another faith by the same Spirit, to another gifts of healing by that one Spirit, to another miraculous powers, to another prophecy, to another distinguishing between spirits, to another speaking in different kinds of tongues, and to still another the interpretation of tongues. All these are the work of one and the same Spirit, and he gives them to each one, just as he determines.
(1 Corinthians 12:7-11)

It was he who gave some to be apostles, some to be prophets, some to be evangelists, and some to be pastors and teachers, to prepare God's people for works of service, so that the body of Christ may be built up until we all reach unity in the faith and in the knowledge of the Son of God and become mature, attaining to the whole measure of the fullness of Christ.
(Ephesians 4:11-13)

If a man's gift is prophesying, let him use it in proportion to his faith. If it is serving, let him serve; if it is teaching, let him teach; if it is encouraging, let him encourage; if it is contributing to the needs of others, let him give generously; if it is leadership, let him govern diligently; if it is showing mercy, let him do it cheerfully.
(Romans 12:6-8)

Each one should use whatever gift he has received to serve others, faithfully administering God's grace in its various forms.
(1 Peter 4:10)

If I have the gift of prophecy and can fathom all mysteries and all knowledge, and if I have a faith that can move mountains, but have not love, I am nothing.
(1 Corinthians 13:2)

His divine power has given us everything we need for life and godliness through our knowledge of him who called us by his own glory and goodness.
(2 Peter 1:3)

GIVING

Freely you have received, freely give.
(Matthew 10:8)

It is more blessed to give than to receive.
(Acts 20:35)

Each man should give what he has decided in his heart to give, not reluctantly or under compulsion, for God loves a cheerful giver.
(2 Corinthians 9:7)

Give, and it will be given to you...For with the measure you use, it will be measured to you.
(Luke 6:38)

Give to the one who asks you, and do not turn away from the one who wants to borrow from you.
(Matthew 5:42)

If anyone has material possessions and sees his brother in need but has no pity on him, how can the love of God be in him?
(1 John 3:17)

Honor the LORD with your wealth, with the firstfruits of all your crops.
(Proverbs 3:9)

A generous man will prosper; he who refreshes others will himself be refreshed.
(Proverbs 11:25)

He who despises his neighbor sins, but blessed is he who is kind to the needy.
(Proverbs 14:21)

He who is kind to the poor lends to the Lord, and he will reward him for what he has done.
(Proverbs 19:17)

If a man shuts his ears to the cry of the poor, he too will cry out and not be answered.
(Proverbs 21:13)

He who gives to the poor will lack nothing, but he who closes his eyes to them receives many curses.
(Proverbs 28:27)

Share with God's people who are in need. Practice hospitality.
(Romans 12:13)

One man gives freely, yet gains even more; another withholds unduly, but comes to poverty.
(Proverbs 11:24)

"Good teacher," he asked, "what must I do to inherit eternal life?"....Jesus looked at him and loved him. *One thing you lack,* he said. *Go, sell everything you have and give to the poor, and you will have treasure in heaven. Then come, follow me.*
(Mark 10:17-21)

If you spend yourselves in behalf of the hungry and satisfy the needs of the oppressed, then your light will rise in the darkness, and your night will become like the noonday.
(Isaiah 58:10)

GOD, ALL KNOWING

See also:
God, All Powerful
God, Present Everywhere

How precious to me are your thoughts, O God! How vast
is the sum of them! Were I to count them, they would
outnumber the grains of sand.
(Psalm 139:17)

For God is greater than our hearts, and he knows everything.
(1 John 3:20)

Great is our Lord and mighty in power; his understanding has no limit.
(Psalm 147:5)

His wisdom is profound, his power is vast.
(Job 9:4)

Nothing in all creation is hidden from God's sight. Everything is uncovered and laid bare before the eyes of him to
whom we must give account.
(Hebrews 4:13)

Does he who implanted the ear not hear? Does he who
formed the eye not see?
(Psalm 94:9)

As the heavens are higher than the earth, so are my ways
higher than your ways and my thoughts than your
thoughts.
(Isaiah 55:9)

I the LORD search the heart and examine the mind, to reward a man according to his conduct, according to what his deeds deserve.
(Jeremiah 17:10)

You have trusted in your wickedness and have said, "No one sees me."
(Isaiah 47:10)

The lamp of the LORD searches the spirit of a man; it searches out his inmost being.
(Proverbs 20:27)

Your nakedness will be exposed and your shame uncovered.
(Isaiah 47:3)

The crucible for silver and the furnace for gold, but the LORD tests the heart.
(Proverbs 17:3)

O LORD, you have searched me and you know me. You know when I sit and when I rise; you perceive my thoughts from afar.
(Psalm 139:1-2)

You discern my going out and my lying down; you are familiar with all my ways.
(Psalm 139:3)

Before a word is on my tongue you know it completely, O LORD.
(Psalm 139:4)

How great are your works, O LORD, how profound your thoughts!
(Psalm 92:5)

GOD, ALL LOVING

| See also:
| Love, By God

God is love. Whoever lives in love lives in God.
(1 John 4:16)

Whoever does not love does not know God, because God
is love.
(1 John 4:8)

How priceless is your unfailing love!
(Psalm 36:7)

Turn, O LORD, and deliver me; save me because of your
unfailing love.
(Psalm 6:4)

May your love and your truth always protect me.
(Psalm 40:11)

For great is your love, reaching to the heavens; your
faithfulness reaches to the skies.
(Psalm 57:10)

The LORD is compassionate and gracious, slow to anger,
abounding in love.
(Psalm 103:8)

The LORD is faithful to all his promises and loving toward
all he has made.
(Psalm 145:13)

The LORD is righteous in all his ways and loving toward
all he has made.
(Psalm 145:17)

Show us your unfailing love, O LORD, and grant us your salvation.
(Psalm 85:7)

I will sing of the LORD's great love forever.
(Psalm 89:1)

I will declare that your love stands firm forever, that you established your faithfulness in heaven itself.
(Psalm 89:2)

For as high as the heavens are above the earth, so great is his love for those who fear him.
(Psalm 103:11)

For the LORD is good and his love endures forever; his faithfulness continues through all generations.
(Psalm 100:5)

GOD, ALL POWERFUL

See also:
Christ, Divinity Of
God, Awesome
God, Eternal
God, First/Last
God, Present Everywhere
Protection
Refuge/Safety
Strength

In his hand is the life of every creature and the breath of all mankind.
(Job 12:10)

He will not grow tired or weary and his understanding no one can fathom.
(Isaiah 40:28)

Be exalted, O LORD, in your strength; we will sing and praise your might.
(Psalm 21:13)

One thing God has spoken, two things have I heard: that you, O God, are strong, and that you, O LORD, are loving.
(Psalm 62:11-12)

You are the God who performs miracles; you display your power among the peoples.
(Psalm 77:14)

Among the gods there is none like you, O Lord; no deeds can compare with yours.
(Psalm 86:8)

See, the Sovereign LORD comes with power, and his arm rules for him.
(Isaiah 40:10)

Mightier than the thunder of the great waters, mightier than the breakers of the sea — the LORD on high is mighty.
(Psalm 93:4)

Surely the nations are like a drop in a bucket; they are regarded as dust on the scales; he weighs the islands as though they were fine dust.
(Isaiah 40:15)

He wraps himself in light as with a garment; he stretches out the heavens like a tent and lays the beams of his upper chambers on their waters.
(Psalm 104:2-3)

Great are the works of the LORD; they are pondered by all who delight in them.
(Psalm 111:2)

Ah, Sovereign LORD, you have made the heavens and the earth by your great power and outstretched arm. Nothing is too hard for you.
(Jeremiah 32:17)

GOD, AWESOME

See also:
God, All Powerful
God, Creator
God, First/Only

How awesome is the LORD Most
High, the great King over all the
earth!
(Psalm 47:2)

Lift your eyes and look to the heavens: Who created all
these?
(Isaiah 40:26)

My own hands stretched out the heavens; I marshaled
their starry hosts.
(Isaiah 45:12)

He determines the number of the stars and calls them
each by name.
(Psalm 147:4)

Can you fathom the mysteries of God? Can you probe
the limits of the Almighty?
(Job 11:7)

As you do not know the path of the wind, or how the
body is formed in a mother's womb, so you cannot understand the work of God, the Maker of all things.
(Ecclesiastes 11:5)

How lovely is your dwelling place, O LORD Almighty! My
soul yearns, even faints, for the courts of the LORD; my
heart and my flesh cry out for the living God.
(Psalm 84:1)

Turn my eyes away from worthless things.
(Psalm 119:37)

Great is the LORD, and most worthy of praise.
(Psalm 48:1)

The LORD has established his throne in heaven, and his kingdom rules over all.
(Psalm 103:19)

For a thousand years in your sight are like a day that has just gone by, or like a watch in the night.
(Psalm 90:4)

Great is the LORD and most worthy of praise; his greatness no one can fathom.
(Psalm 145:3)

They will speak of the glorious splendor of your majesty, and I will meditate on your wonderful works.
(Psalm 145:5)

Let them praise your great and awesome name — he is holy.
(Psalm 99:3)

Let everything that has breath praise the LORD. Praise the LORD.
(Psalm 150:6)

GOD, CREATOR

See also:
Christ, Divinity Of
Christ, Identity Of
God, All Powerful
God, Awesome

In the beginning God created the heavens and the earth.
(Genesis 1:1)

By faith we understand that the universe was formed at God's command, so that what is seen was not made out of what was visible.
(Hebrews 11:3)

But God made the earth by his power; he founded the world by his wisdom and stretched out the heavens by his understanding.
(Jeremiah 10:12)

For he spoke, and it came to be; he commanded and it stood firm.
(Psalm 33:9)

The heavens declare the glory of God; the skies proclaim the work of his hands.
(Psalm 19:1)

The earth is the LORD's, and everything in it, the world, and all who live in it; for he founded it upon the seas and established it upon the waters.
(Psalm 24:1-2)

"It is I who made the earth and created mankind upon it."
(Isaiah 45:12)

By the word of the LORD were the heavens made, their starry host by the breath of his mouth.
(Psalm 33:6)

In his hands are the depths of the earth, and the mountain peaks belong to him.
(Psalm 95:4)

The day is yours, and yours also the night; you established the sun and moon.
(Psalm 74:16)

It was you who set all the boundaries of the earth; you made both summer and winter.
(Psalm 74:17)

The sea is his, for he made it, and his hands formed the dry land.
(Psalm 95:5)

The LORD God formed the man from the dust of the ground and breathed into his nostrils the breath of life, and the man became a living being.
(Genesis 2:7)

He chose to give us birth through the word of truth, that we might be a kind of first-fruits of all he created.
(James 1:18)

Surely God is my help; the Lord is the one who sustains me.
(Psalm 54:4)

For in him we live and move and have our being.
(Acts 17:28)

We are the clay, you are the potter; we are all the work of your hand.
(Isaiah 64:8)

For every house is built by someone, but God is the builder of everything.
(Hebrews 3:4)

For you created all things, and by your will they were created and have their being.
(Revelation 4:11)

For from him and through him and to him are all things. To him be the glory forever! Amen
(Romans 11:36)

GOD, ETERNAL

See also:
Christ, Divinity Of
Christ, Identity Of
God, First/Only

Do you not know? Have you not heard? The LORD is the everlasting God, the Creator of the ends of the earth.
(Isaiah 40:28)

Your throne was established long ago; you are from all eternity.
(Psalm 93:2)

Before the mountains were born or you brought forth the earth and the world, from everlasting to everlasting you are God.
(Psalm 90:2)

Your faithfulness continues through all generations; you established the earth, and it endures.
(Psalm 119:90)

The LORD is King for ever and ever.
(Psalm 10:16)

I know that everything God does will endure forever; nothing can be added to it and nothing taken from it.
(Ecclesiastes 3:14)

Your throne, O God, will last for ever and ever.
(Psalm 45:6)

With the Lord a day is like a thousand years, and a thousand years are like a day.
(2 Peter 3:8)

But you remain the same, and your years will never end.
(Psalm 102:27)

He rules forever by his power.
(Psalm 66:7)

For this God is our God for ever and ever; he will be our
guide even to the end.
(Psalm 48:14)

Your righteousness is everlasting and your law is true.
(Psalm 119:142)

*My Father is always at his work to this very day, and I, too, am
working.*
(John 5:17)

Now to the King eternal, immortal, invisible, the only
God, be honor and glory for ever and ever. Amen.
(1 Timothy 1:17)

GOD, FIRST/ ONLY

See also:
Christ, Divinity Of
Christ, Identity Of
God, All Powerful
God, Eternal

Hear, O Israel: The LORD our God,
the LORD is one.
(Deuteronomy 6:4)

Fear the LORD your God, serve him only and take your
oaths in his name.
(Deuteronomy 6:13)

You shall have no foreign god among you; you shall not
bow down to an alien god.
(Psalm 81:9)

Acknowledge and take to heart this day that the LORD is
God in heaven above and on the earth below. There is no
other.
(Deuteronomy 4:39)

For there is one God and one mediator between God and
men, the man Christ Jesus, who gave himself as a ransom
for all men — the testimony given in its proper time.
(1 Timothy 2:5-6)

I, even I, am the LORD, and apart from me there is no
savior.
(Isaiah 43:11)

I am the first and I am the last; apart from me there is no
God.
(Isaiah 44:6)

I am the LORD, and there is no other.
(Isaiah 45:5)

Before me every knee will bow; by me every tongue will swear.
(Isaiah 45:23)

But the LORD is the true God; he is the living God, the eternal King.
(Jeremiah 10:10)

For you are great and do marvelous deeds; you alone are God.
(Psalm 86:10)

For you alone are holy.
(Revelation 15:4)

Do you think I came to bring peace on earth? No, I tell you, but division.
(Luke 12:51)

No one can serve two masters.
(Matthew 6:24)

I did not come to bring peace, but a sword.
(Matthew 10:34)

From now on there will be five in one family divided against each other, three against two and two against three.
(Luke 12:52)

For I have come to turn "a man against his father, a daughter against her mother, a daughter-in-law against her mother-in-law — a man's enemies will be the members of his own household."
(Matthew 10:35-36)

I have come to bring fire on the earth, and how I wish it were already kindled!
(Luke 12:49)

GOD, PRESENT EVERYWHERE

> **See also:**
> God, All Knowing

"Am I only a God nearby," declares the LORD, "and not a God far away?"
(Jeremiah 23:23)

"Can anyone hide in secret places so that I cannot see him?" declares the LORD. "Do not I fill heaven and earth?" declares the LORD.
(Jeremiah 23:24)

If I say, "Surely the darkness will hide me and the light become night around me," even the darkness will not be dark to you; the night will shine like day, for the darkness is as light to you.
(Psalm 139:11-12)

Where can I go from your Spirit? Where can I flee from your presence?
(Psalm 139:7)

If I go up to the heavens, you are there; if I make my bed in the depths, you are there.
(Psalm 139:8)

If I rise on the wings of the dawn, if I settle on the far side of the sea, even there your hand will guide me, your right hand will hold me fast.
(Psalm 139:9-10)

The eyes of the LORD are everywhere, keeping watch on the wicked and the good.
(Proverbs 15:3)

My eyes are on all their ways; they are not hidden from me, nor is their sin concealed from my eyes.
(Jeremiah 16:17)

From the heaven the LORD looks down and sees all mankind; from his dwelling place he watches all who live on earth — he who forms the hearts of all, who considers everything they do.
(Psalm 33:13-15)

GOSSIP

See also:
Communication
Lying
Slander
Swearing

The words of a gossip are like choice morsels; they go down to a man's inmost parts.
(Proverbs 18:8)

The mouth of the wicked gulps down evil.
(Proverbs 19:28)

A gossip betrays a confidence, but a trustworthy man keeps a secret.
(Proverbs 11:13)

Do not spread false reports. Do not help a wicked man by being a malicious witness.
(Exodus 23:1)

A perverse man stirs up dissension, and a gossip separates close friends.
(Proverbs 16:28)

And not only do they become idlers, but also gossips and busybodies, saying things they ought not to.
(1 Timothy 5:13)

He who covers over an offense promotes love, but whoever repeats the matter separates close friends.
(Proverbs 17:9)

A gossip betrays a confidence; so avoid a man who talks too much.
(Proverbs 20:19)

A wicked man listens to evil lips; a liar pays attention to a malicious tongue.
(Proverbs 17:4)

Without wood a fire goes out; without gossip a quarrel
dies down.
(Proverbs 26:20)

*For by your words you will be acquitted, and by your words
you will be condemned.*
(Matthew 12:37)

GRACE

See also:
Action
Belief
Eternal Life
Faith
Salvation

It is by grace you have been saved.
(Ephesians 2:5)

But join with me in suffering for the gospel, by the power of God, who has saved us and called us to a holy life — not because of anything we have done but because of his own purpose and grace.
(2 Timothy 1:8-9)

This grace was given us in Christ Jesus before the beginning of time, but it has now been revealed through the appearing of our Savior, Christ Jesus, who has destroyed death and has brought life and immortality to light through the gospel.
(2 Timothy 1:9-10)

In him we have redemption through his blood, the forgiveness of sins, in accordance with the riches of God's grace that he lavished on us with all wisdom and understanding.
(Ephesians 1:7-8)

And God raised us up with Christ and seated us with him in the heavenly realms in Christ Jesus, in order that in the coming ages he might show the incomparable riches of his grace, expressed in his kindness to us in Christ Jesus.
(Ephesians 2:6-7)

For it is by grace you have been saved, through faith — and this not from yourselves, it is the gift of God — not by works, so that no one can boast.
(Ephesians 2:8-9)

A man is not justified by observing the law, but by faith in Jesus Christ.
(Galatians 2:16)

The life I live in the body, I live by faith in the Son of God, who loved me and gave himself for me. I do not set aside the grace of God, for if righteousness could be gained through the law, Christ died for nothing!
(Galatians 2:20-21)

Clearly no one is justified before God by the law, because, "The righteous will live by faith."
(Galatians 3:11)

For sin shall not be your master, because you are not under law, but under grace.
(Romans 6:14)

Therefore, since we have been justified through faith, we have peace with God through our Lord Jesus Christ, through whom we have gained access by faith into this grace in which we now stand.
(Romans 5:1)

For if, by the trespass of the one man, death reigned through that one man, how much more will those who receive God's abundant provision of grace and of the gift of righteousness reign in life through the one man, Jesus Christ.
(Romans 5:17)

But where sin increased, grace increased all the more, so that, just as sin reigned in death, so also grace might reign through righteousness to bring eternal life through Jesus Christ our Lord.
(Romans 5:20-21)

But thanks be to God that, though you used to be slaves to sin....You have been set free from sin and have become slaves to righteousness.
(Romans 6:17-18)

For the grace of God that brings salvation has appeared to all men. It teaches us to say "No" to ungodliness and worldly passions, and to live self-controlled, upright and godly lives.
(Titus 2:11-12)

But when the kindness and love of God our Savior appeared, he saved us, not because of righteous things we had done, but because of his mercy.
(Titus 3:4-5)

He saved us through the washing of rebirth and renewal by the Holy Spirit, whom he poured out on us generously through Jesus Christ our Savior, so that, having been justified by his grace, we might become heirs having the hope of eternal life.
(Titus 3:5-7)

GREEDY/STINGY

See also:
Envy/Jealousy
Giving
Money
Poverty
Riches, Beware Of
Riches, True
Worldly

Watch out! Be on guard against all kinds of greed; a man's life does not consist in the abundance of his possessions.
(Luke 12:15)

A greedy man brings trouble to his family.
(Proverbs 15:27)

All man's efforts are for his mouth, yet his appetite is never satisfied.
(Ecclesiastes 6:7)

Death and Destruction are never satisfied, and neither are the eyes of man.
(Proverbs 27:20)

As goods increase, so do those who consume them. And what benefit are they to the owner except to feast his eyes on them?
(Ecclesiastes 5:11)

Better one handful with tranquillity than two handfuls with toil and chasing after the wind.
(Ecclesiastes 4:6)

A greedy man stirs up dissension, but he who trusts the Lord will prosper.
(Proverbs 28:25)

A stingy man is eager to get rich and is unaware that poverty awaits him.
(Proverbs 28:22)

Do not eat the food of a stingy man, do not crave his delicacies; for he is the kind of man who is always thinking about cost. "Eat and drink," he says to you, but his heart is not with you.
(Proverbs 23:6-7)

What causes fights and quarrels among you? Don't they come from your desires that battle within you? You want something but don't get it. You kill and covet, but you cannot have what you want. You quarrel and fight. You do not have, because you do not ask God.
(James 4:1-2)

When you ask, you do not receive, because you ask with wrong motives, that you may spend what you get on your pleasures.
(James 4:3)

Do not exploit the poor because they are poor.
(Proverbs 22:22)

He who oppresses the poor to increase his wealth and he who gives gifts to the rich — both come to poverty.
(Proverbs 22:16)

Turn my heart toward your statutes and not toward selfish gain.
(Psalm 119:36)

Naked a man comes from his mother's womb, and as he comes, so he departs. He takes nothing from his labor that he can carry in his hand.
(Ecclesiastes 5:15)

GRIEF

See also:
Death/Dying
Heaven
Help
Hopeless
Psalm 23
Refuge/Safety
Sorrow
Strength
Suffering
Weakness

The LORD is close to the broken-hearted and saves those who are crushed in spirit.
(Psalm 34:18)

The Sovereign LORD will wipe away the tears from all faces.
(Isaiah 25:8)

He heals the brokenhearted and binds up their wounds.
(Psalm 147:3)

Surely he took up our infirmities and carried our sorrows.
(Isaiah 53:4)

My soul is weary with sorrow; strengthen me according to your word.
(Psalm 119:28)

Death is the destiny of every man; the living should take this to heart.
(Ecclesiastes 7:2)

Brothers, we do not want you to be ignorant about those who fall asleep, or to grieve like the rest of men, who have no hope.
(1 Thessalonians 4:13)

We believe that Jesus died and rose again and so we believe that God will bring with Jesus those who have fallen asleep in him.
(1 Thessalonians 4:14)

For this very reason, Christ died and returned to life so that he might be the Lord of both the dead and the living.
(Romans 14:9)

When the perishable has been clothed with the imperishable, and the mortal with immortality, then the saying that is written will come true: "Death has been swallowed up in victory."
(1 Corinthians 15:54)

Why are you downcast, O my soul? Why so disturbed within me? Put your hope in God, for I will yet praise him, my Savior and my God.
(Psalm 43:5)

He will have no fear of bad news; his heart is steadfast, trusting in the LORD.
(Psalm 112:7)

There is a time for everything, and a season for every activity under heaven: a time to be born and a time to die ... a time to weep and a time to laugh...a time to mourn and a time to dance...
(Ecclesiastes 3:1-4)

Rejoice with those who rejoice; mourn with those who mourn.
(Romans 12:15)

Blessed are you who weep now, for you will laugh.
(Luke 6:21)

You turned my wailing into dancing; you removed my sackcloth and clothed me with joy, that my heart may sing to you and not be silent.
(Psalm 30:11-12)

They will enter Zion with singing; everlasting joy will crown their heads. Gladness and joy will overtake them, and sorrow and sighing will flee away.
(Isaiah 35:10)

GUIDANCE

See also:
Discipline
Wisdom

I will instruct you and teach you in the way
you should go; I will counsel you and
watch over you.
(Psalm 32:8)

I know, O LORD, that a man's life is not his own; it is not
for man to direct his steps.
(Jeremiah 10:23)

Teach me your way, O LORD, and I will walk in your truth.
(Psalm 86:11)

Show me the way I should go, for to you I lift up my soul.
(Psalm 143:8)

Send forth your light and your truth, let them guide me;
let them bring me to your holy mountain, to the place
where you dwell.
(Psalm 43:3)

Teach me your way, O LORD; lead me in a straight path
because of my oppressors.
(Psalm 27:11)

Direct my footsteps according to your word; let no sin
rule over me.
(Psalm 119:133)

Since you are my rock and my fortress, for the sake of
your name lead and guide me.
(Psalm 31:3)

Lead me, O LORD, in your righteousness because of my
enemies — make straight your way before me.
(Psalm 5:8)

To God belong wisdom and power; counsel and
understanding are his.
(Job 12:13)

When my spirit grows faint within me, it is you who
know my way.
(Psalm 142:3)

You broaden the path beneath me, so that my ankles do
not turn.
(Psalm 18:36)

You have made known to me the path of life.
(Psalm 16:11)

He guides me in paths of righteousness for his name's sake.
(Psalm 23:3)

The LORD will guide you always; he will satisfy your
needs in a sun-scorched land and will strengthen your
frame.
(Isaiah 58:11)

You guide me with your counsel, and afterward you will
take me into glory.
(Psalm 73:24)

GUILT/SHAME

My guilt has overwhelmed me like a burden too heavy to bear.
(Psalm 38:4)

See also:
Christ, Mission Of
Confession
Darkness
Depression, Symptoms Of
Forgive
Forgiveness
Light

I am troubled by my sin.
(Psalm 38:18)

Forgive my hidden faults.
(Psalm 19:12)

Remember not the sins of my youth and my rebellious ways.
(Psalm 25:7)

Save me from all my transgressions.
(Psalm 39:8)

Hide your face from my sins and blot out all my iniquity.
(Psalm 51:9)

When we were overwhelmed by sins, you forgave our transgressions.
(Psalm 65:3)

Then I acknowledged my sin to you and did not cover up my iniquity. I said, "I will confess my transgressions to the LORD" — and you forgave the guilt of my sin.
(Psalm 32:5)

If you, O LORD, kept a record of sins, O Lord, who could stand? But with you there is forgiveness.
(Psalm 130:3-4)

It is not the healthy who need a doctor, but the sick. I have not come to call the righteous, but sinners.
(Mark 2:17)

Though your sins be like scarlet, they shall be as white as snow; though they are as red as crimson, they shall be like wool.
(Isaiah 1:18)

Cleanse me with hyssop, and I will be clean; wash me, and I will be whiter than snow.
(Psalm 51:7)

You were washed, you were sanctified, you were justified in the name of the Lord Jesus Christ and by the Spirit of our God.
(1 Corinthians 6:11)

We all, like sheep, have gone astray, each of us has turned to his own way; and the LORD has laid on him the iniquity of us all.
(Isaiah 53:6)

I have swept away your offenses like a cloud, your sins like the morning mist. Return to me, for I have redeemed you.
(Isaiah 44:22)

I, even I, am he who blots out your transgressions, for my own sake, and remembers your sins no more.
(Isaiah 43:25)

Blessed is he whose transgressions are forgiven, whose sins are covered.
(Psalm 32:1)

HARDSHIP

See also:
Discipline
Guidance
Prayer, Answers To
Sickness
Strength
Suffering
Tired
Troubles
Weakness

The fire will test the quality of each man's work.
(1 Corinthians 3:13)

Be joyful always; pray continually; give thanks in all circumstances, for this is God's will for you in Christ Jesus.
(1 Thessalonians 5:16-18)

Endure hardship with us like a good soldier of Christ Jesus.
(2 Timothy 2:3)

When times are good, be happy; but when times are bad, consider: God has made the one as well as the other.
(Ecclesiastes 7:14)

Light is sweet, and it pleases the eyes to see the sun. However many years a man may live, let him enjoy them all. But let him remember the days of darkness, for they will be many.
(Ecclesiastes 11:7-8)

Endure hardship as discipline; God is treating you as sons. For what son is not disciplined by his father?
(Hebrews 12:7)

Blessed is the man who perseveres under trial, because when he has stood the test, he will receive the crown of life that God has promised to those who love him.
(James 1:12)

I will continue to rejoice, for I know that through your prayers and the help given by the Spirit of Jesus Christ, what has happened to me will turn out for my deliverance.
(Philippians 1:18-19)

Praise be to the Lord, to God our Savior, who daily bears our burdens.
(Psalm 68:19)

HATRED

See also:
Anger
Forgive
Judgmental
Love, For Others
Peace
Vengeance

Do not hate your brother in
your heart.
(Leviticus 19:17)

Anyone who claims to be in
the light but hates his brother
is still in the darkness.
(1 John 2:9)

If anyone says, "I love God," yet hates his brother, he is a
liar. For anyone who does not love his brother, whom he
has seen, cannot love God, whom he has not seen.
(1 John 4:20)

But whoever hates his brother is in the darkness and
walks around in the darkness; he does not know where
he is going, because the darkness has blinded him.
(1 John 2:11)

Get rid of all bitterness, rage and anger, brawling and
slander, along with every form of malice.
(Ephesians 4:31)

Do not drag me away with the wicked, with those who
do evil, who speak cordially with their neighbors but
harbor malice in their hearts.
(Psalm 28:3)

Therefore, rid yourselves of all malice and all deceit,
hypocrisy, envy and slander of every kind.
(1 Peter 2:1)

If your brother sins, rebuke him, and if he repents, forgive him.
(Luke 17:3)

Hatred stirs up dissension, but love covers over all
wrongs.
(Proverbs 10:12)

*You have heard that it was said, "Love your neighbor and hate
your enemy." But I tell you: Love your enemies and pray for
those who persecute you, that you may be sons of your Father
in heaven.*
(Matthew 5:43-44)

HEAVEN

See also:
Belief
Eternal Life
Hell
Salvation
Second Coming

No eye has seen, no ear has heard,
no mind has conceived what God has
prepared for those who love him.
(1 Corinthians 2:9)

I lift up my eyes to you, to you whose throne is in
heaven.
(Psalm 123:1)

I see heaven open and the Son of Man standing at the
right hand of God."
(Acts 7:56)

When I awake, I will be satisfied with seeing your
likeness.
(Psalm 17:15)

I love the house where you live, O LORD, the place where
your glory dwells.
(Psalm 26:8)

Better is one day in your courts than a thousand else-
where; I would rather be a doorkeeper in the house of my
God than dwell in the tents of the wicked.
(Psalm 84:10)

Blessed are those who dwell in your house; they are ever
praising you.
(Psalm 84:4)

One thing I ask of the LORD, this is what I seek: that I may
dwell in the house of the LORD all the days of my life, to gaze
upon the beauty of the LORD and to seek him in his temple.
(Psalm 27:4)

Where I am going, you cannot follow now, but you will follow later.
(John 13:36)

*In my Father's house are many rooms; if it were not so, I would
have told you. I am going there to prepare a place for you.*
(John 14:2)

*And I confer on you a kingdom, just as my Father conferred
one on me, so that you may eat and drink at my table in my
kingdom and sit on thrones, judging the twelve tribes of Israel.*
(Luke 22:29-30)

*Father, I want those you have given me to be with me where I
am, and to see my glory, the glory you have given me because
you loved me before the creation of the world*
(John 17:24)

Your kingdom is an everlasting kingdom, and your
dominion endures through all generations.
(Psalm 145:13)

In keeping with his promise we are looking forward to a
new heaven and a new earth, the home of righteousness.
(2 Peter 3:13)

For here we do not have an enduring city, but we are
looking for the city that is to come.
(Hebrews 13:14)

The wall was made of jasper, and the city of pure gold, as
pure as glass. The foundations of the city walls were
decorated with every kind of precious stone.
(Revelation 21:18-19)

The twelve gates were twelve pearls, each gate made of a
single pearl. The great street of the city was of pure gold,
like transparent glass.
(Revelation 21:21)

The city does not need the sun or the moon to shine on it, for the glory of God gives it light, and the Lamb is its lamp.
(Revelation 21:23)

On no day will its gates ever be shut, for there will be no night there.
(Revelation 21:25)

Nothing impure will ever enter it, nor will anyone who does what is shameful or deceitful, but only those whose names are written in the Lamb's book of life.
(Revelation 21:27)

They will see his face, and his name will be on their foreheads.
(Revelation 22:4)

There will be no more night. They will not need the light of a lamp or the light of the sun, for the Lord God will give them light. And they will reign for ever and ever.
(Revelation 22:5)

Rejoice that your names are written in heaven.
(Luke 10:20)

HELL

See also:
Denial
Second Coming
Sin, Consequences Of
Unbelief

*The Son of Man will send out of his
kingdom everything that causes sin
and all who do evil. They will throw
them into the fiery furnace, where
there will be weeping and gnashing
of teeth.*
(Matthew 13:41-42)

His winnowing fork is in his hand to clear his threshing
floor and to gather the wheat into his barn, but he will
burn up the chaff with unquenchable fire.
(Luke 3:17)

*Then he will say to those on his left, "Depart from me, you who are
cursed, into the eternal fire prepared for the devil and his angels."*
(Matthew 25:41)

He will punish those who do not know God and do not
obey the gospel of our Lord Jesus.
(2 Thessalonians 1:8)

They will be punished with everlasting destruction and
shut out from the presence of the Lord and from the
majesty of his power on the day he comes to be glorified
in his holy people and to be marveled at among all those
who have believed.
(2 Thessalonians 1:9-10)

As heat and drought snatch away the melted snow, so
the grave snatches away those who have sinned.
(Job 24:19)

Whatever your hand finds to do, do it with all your might, for in the grave, where you are going, there is neither working nor planning nor knowledge nor wisdom.
(Ecclesiastes 9:10)

They perish because they refused to love the truth and so be saved. For this reason God sends them a powerful delusion so that they will believe the lie and so that all will be condemned who have not **believed** the truth but have delighted in wickedness.
(2 Thessalonians 2:10-12)

If your hand causes you to sin, cut it off. It is better for you to enter life maimed than with two hands to go into hell, where the fire never goes out.
(Mark 9:43)

And if your eye causes you to sin, pluck it out. It is better for you to enter the kingdom of God with one eye than to have two eyes and be thrown into hell, where "their worm does not die, and the fire is not quenched."
(Mark 9:47)

In hell, where he was in torment, he looked up and saw Abraham far away, with Lazarus by his side. So he called to him, "Father Abraham, have pity on me and send Lazarus to dip the tip of his finger in water and cool my tongue, because I am in agony in this fire."
(Luke 16:23-24)

Son, remember that in your lifetime you received your good things, while Lazarus received bad things, but now he is comforted here and you are in agony.
(Luke 16:25)

Between us and you a great chasm has been fixed, so that those who want to go from here to you cannot, nor can anyone cross over from there to us.
(Luke 16:26)

HELP

See also:
God, All Powerful
Guidance
Mercy
Prayer, Answers To
Protection
Strength
Refuge/Safety
Trust
Weakness

I lift up my eyes to the hills —
where does my help come
from?
(Psalm 121:1)

My help comes from the LORD,
the Maker of heaven and earth.
(Psalm 121:2)

Arise, LORD! Lift up your hand, O God. Do not forget the
helpless.
(Psalm 10:12)

The Lord knows how to rescue godly men from trials.
(2 Peter 2:9)

Come quickly to help me, O Lord my Savior.
(Psalm 38:22)

You come to the help of those who gladly do right, who
remember your ways.
(Isaiah 64:5)

Help me, O LORD my God; save me in accordance with
your love.
(Psalm 109:26)

I, even I, am he who comforts you.
(Isaiah 51:12)

Rescue me and deliver me in your righteousness; turn
your ear to me and save me.
(Psalm 71:2)

For I am the LORD, your God, who takes hold of your
right hand and says to you, Do not fear; I will help you.
(Isaiah 41:13)

Guard my life and rescue me; let me not be put to shame,
for I take refuge in you.
(Psalm 25:20)

When I said, "My foot is slipping," your love, O LORD,
supported me.
(Psalm 94:18)

Be pleased, O LORD, to save me; O LORD, come quickly to
help me.
(Psalm 40:13)

Because you are my help, I sing in the shadow of your wings.
(Psalm 63:7)

Listen to my cry, for I am in desperate need; rescue me from
those who pursue me, for they are too strong for me.
(Psalm 142:6)

I have set the Lord always before me. Because he is at my
right hand, I will not be shaken.
(Psalm 16:8)

Rise up and help us; redeem us because of your unfailing love.
(Psalm 44:26)

My eyes are ever on the LORD, for only he will release my
feet from the snare.
(Psalm 25:15)

Save us and help us with your right hand, that those you
love may be delivered.
(Psalm 60:5)

You are my help and my deliverer; O my God, do not delay.
(Psalm 40:17)

May the LORD answer you when you are in distress; may
the name of the God of Jacob protect you.
(Psalm 20:1)

When I was in great need, he saved me.
(Psalm 116:6)

I was pushed back and about to fall, but the LORD helped
me.
(Psalm 118:13)

Blessed is he whose help is the God of Jacob, whose hope
is in the LORD his God, the Maker of heaven and earth,
the sea, and everything in them — the LORD, who remains faithful forever.
(Psalm 146:5-6)

HOLY SPIRIT

See also:
Guidance
Holy Spirit, Pentecost

God has poured out his love into
our hearts by the Holy Spirit,
whom he has given us.
(Romans 5:5)

And this is how we know that he lives in us: We know it
by the Spirit he gave us.
(1 John 3:24)

We know that we live in him and he in us, because he has
given us of his Spirit.
(1 John 4:13)

Because you are sons, God sent the Spirit of his Son into
our hearts, the Spirit who calls out, "Abba, Father."
(Galatians 4:6)

Having believed, you were marked in him with a seal,
the promised Holy Spirit, who is a deposit guaranteeing
our inheritance until the redemption of those who are
God's possession — to the praise of his glory.
(Ephesians 1:13-14)

The Spirit himself testifies with our spirit that we are
God's children.
(Romans 8:16)

The fruit of the Spirit is love, joy, peace, patience, kindness, goodness, faithfulness, gentleness, and self-control.
(Galatians 5:22)

And if anyone does not have the Spirit of Christ, he does
not belong to Christ.
(Romans 8:9)

And if the Spirit of him who raised Jesus from the dead is living in you, he who raised Christ from the dead will also give life to your mortal bodies through his Spirit, who lives in you.
(Romans 8:11)

The Spirit gives life; the flesh counts for nothing.
(John 6:63)

For this is the reason the gospel was preached even to those who are now dead, so that they might be judged according to men in regard to the body, but live according to God in regard to the spirit.
(1 Peter 4:6)

The Spirit searches all things, even the deep things of God. For who among men knows the thoughts of a man except the man's spirit within him? In the same way no one knows the thoughts of God except the Spirit of God.
(1 Corinthians 2:10-11)

We have not received the spirit of the world but the Spirit who is from God, that we may understand what God has freely given us.
(1 Corinthians 2:12)

This is what we speak, not in words taught us by human wisdom but in words taught by the Spirit, expressing spiritual truths in spiritual words.
(1 Corinthians 2:13)

The man without the Spirit does not accept the things that come from the Spirit of God, for they are foolishness to him, and he cannot understand them, because they are spiritually discerned.
(1 Corinthians 2:14)

Like newborn babies, crave pure spiritual milk, so that by it you may grow up in your salvation, now that you have tasted that the Lord is good.
(1 Peter 2:2)

And do not grieve the Holy Spirit of God, with whom you were sealed for the day of redemption.
(Ephesians 4:30)

Therefore I tell you that no one who is speaking by the Spirit of God says, "Jesus be cursed," and no one can say, "Jesus is Lord," except by the Holy Spirit.
(1 Corinthians 12:3)

I pray that out of his glorious riches he may strengthen you with power through his Spirit in your inner being, so that Christ may dwell in your hearts through faith.
(Ephesians 3:16-17)

May the grace of the Lord Jesus Christ, and the love of God, and the fellowship of the Holy Spirit be with you all.
(2 Corinthians 13:14)

HOLY SPIRIT, PENTECOST

See also:
Gifts, Spiritual
Holy Spirit

And I will ask the Father, and he will give you another Counselor to be with you forever—the Spirit of truth.
(John 14:16-17)

The world cannot accept him, because it neither sees him nor knows him. But you know him, for he lives with you and will be in you.
(John 14:17)

All this I have spoken while still with you. But the Counselor, the Holy Spirit, whom the Father will send in my name, will teach you all things and will remind you of everything I have said to you.
(John 14:25-26)

When the Counselor comes, whom I will send to you from the Father, the Spirit of truth who goes out from the Father, he will testify about me.
(John 15:26)

Unless I go away, the Counselor will not come to you; but if I go, I will send him to you.
(John 16:7)

When he comes, he will convict the world of guilt in regard to sin and righteousness and judgment.
(John 16:8)

But when he, the Spirit of truth, comes, he will guide you into all truth.
(John 16:13)

*He will bring glory to me by taking from what is mine and
making it known to you.*
(John 16:14)

When the day of Pentecost came, they were all together
in one place.
(Acts 2:1)

Suddenly a sound like the blowing of a violent wind
came from heaven and filled the whole house where they
were sitting.
(Acts 2:2)

They saw what seemed to be tongues of fire that separated and came to rest on each of them.
(Acts 2:3)

All of them were filled with the Holy Spirit and began to
speak in other tongues as the Spirit enabled them.
(Acts 2:4)

After they prayed, the place they were meeting was
shaken. And they were all filled with the Holy Spirit and
spoke the word of God boldly.
(Acts 4:31)

Repent and be baptized, every one of you, in the name of
Jesus Christ for the forgiveness of your sins. And you
will receive the gift of the Holy Spirit.
(Acts 2:38)

HOMOSEXUALITY

See also:
Lust
Promiscuity
Sex, Normal
Sex, Perverted

Do not lie with a man as one lies with a woman; that is detestable.
(Leviticus 18:22)

Do you not know that the wicked will not inherit the kingdom of God? Do not be deceived: Neither the sexually immoral nor idolaters nor adulterers nor male prostitutes nor homosexual offenders nor thieves nor the greedy nor drunkards nor slanderers nor swindlers will inherit the kingdom of God.
(1 Corinthians 6:9-10)

They called to Lot, "Where are the men who came to you tonight? Bring them out to us so that we can have sex with them." Lot went outside to meet them and shut the door behind him and said, "No, my friends. Don't do this wicked thing."
(Genesis 19:5-7)

Because of this, God gave them over to shameful lusts. Even their women exchanged natural relations for unnatural ones.
(Romans 1:26)

In the same way the men also abandoned natural relations with women and were inflamed with lust for one another.
(Romans 1:27)

Men committed indecent acts with other men, and received in themselves the due penalty for their perversion.
(Romans 1:27)

The look on their faces testifies against them; they parade their sin like Sodom; they do not hide it. Woe to them! They have brought disaster upon themselves.
(Isaiah 3:9)

For a man's ways are in full view of the LORD, and he examines all his paths.
(Proverbs 5:21)

No one who lives in him keeps on sinning. No one who continues to sin has either seen him or known him.
(1 John 3:6)

HOPELESS

See also:
God, All Powerful
God, Awesome
God, Creator
Guidance
Prayer, Answers To
Strength
Tired
Weakness

Anyone who is among the living has hope.
(Ecclesiastes 9:4)

Why are you downcast, O my soul? Why so disturbed within me? Put your hope in God, for I will yet praise him, my Savior and my God.
(Psalm 42:5)

Praise be to the God and Father of our Lord Jesus Christ! In his great mercy he has given us new birth into a living hope through the resurrection of Jesus Christ form the dead.
(1 Peter 1:3)

May our Lord Jesus Christ himself and God our Father, who loved us and by his grace gave us eternal encouragement and good hope, encourage your hearts and strengthen you in every good deed and word.
(2 Thessalonians 2:16-17)

Find rest, O my soul, in God alone; my hope comes from him.
(Psalm 62:5)

Sustain me according to your promise, and I will live; do not let my hopes be dashed.
(Psalm 119:116)

May your unfailing love rest upon us, O LORD, even as we put our hope in you.
(Psalm 33:22)

For you have been my hope, O Sovereign LORD, my
confidence since my youth.
(Psalm 71:5)

In your name I will hope, for your name is good.
(Psalm 52:9)

No one whose hope is in you will ever be put to shame.
(Psalm 25:3)

You are God my Savior, and my hope is in you all day
long.
(Psalm 25:5)

You answer us with awesome deeds of righteousness, O
God our Savior, the hope of all the ends of the earth and
of the farthest seas.
(Psalm 65:5)

Those who hope in the LORD will inherit the land.
(Psalm 37:9)

But hope that is seen is no hope at all. Who hopes for
what he already has? But if we hope for what we do not
yet have, we wait for it patiently.
(Romans 8:24-25)

I have put my hope in your word.
(Psalm 119:74)

For everything that was written in the past was written to
teach us, so that through endurance and the encouragement of the Scriptures we might have hope.
(Romans 15:4)

I pray also that the eyes of your heart may be enlightened in
order that you may know the hope to which he has called

you, the riches of his glorious inheritance in the saints, and
his incomparably great power for us who believe.
(Ephesians 1:18-19)

There is one body and one Spirit — just as you were
called to one hope when you were called — one Lord,
one faith, one baptism; one God and Father of all, who is
over all and through all and in all.
(Ephesians 4:4-6)

Therefore, since we have such a hope, we are very bold.
(2 Corinthians 3:12)

Always be prepared to give an answer to everyone who
asks you to give the reason for the hope that you have.
But do this with gentleness and respect, keeping a clear
conscience, so that those who speak maliciously against
your good behavior in Christ may be ashamed of their
slander.
(1 Peter 3:15-16)

But as for me, I will always have hope; I will praise you
more and more.
(Psalm 71:14)

May the God of hope fill you with all joy and peace as
you trust in him, so that you may overflow with hope by
the power of the Holy Spirit.
(Romans 15:13)

HUMILITY

See also:
Boastful
Conceit
God, All Powerful
God, Awesome
Intelligence
Prejudice
Pride
Servant
Sinful Nature
Wisdom

Humble yourselves before the
Lord, and he will lift you up.
(James 4:10)

This is the one I esteem: He who
is humble and contrite in spirit,
and trembles at my word.
(Isaiah 66:2)

For everyone who exalts himself will be humbled, and he who
humbles himself will be exalted.
(Luke 14:11)

He chose the lowly things of this world and the despised
things — and the things that are not — to nullify the
things that are, so that no one may boast before him.
(1 Corinthians 1:28-29)

So neither he who plants nor he who waters is anything,
but only God, who makes things grow.
(1 Corinthians 3:7)

Do nothing out of selfish ambition or vain conceit, but in
humility consider others better than yourselves.
(Philippians 2:3)

Honor one another above yourselves.
(Romans 12:10)

All of you, clothe yourselves with humility toward one
another, because, "God opposes the proud, but gives
grace to the humble."
(1 Peter 5:5)

For we do not preach ourselves, but Jesus Christ as Lord, and ourselves as your servants for Jesus' sake.
(2 Corinthians 4:5)

So you also, when you have done everything you were told to do, should say, "We are unworthy servants; we have only done our duty."
(Luke 17:10)

Your attitude should be the same as that of Christ Jesus: Who, being in very nature God, did not consider equality with God something to be grasped, but made himself nothing, taking the very nature of a servant, being made in human likeness.
(Philippians 2:5-7)

Humility and fear of the LORD bring wealth and honor and life.
(Proverbs 22:4)

You save the humble but bring low those whose eyes are haughty.
(Psalm 18:27)

But the meek will inherit the land and enjoy great peace.
(Psalm 37:11)

HUSBANDS

See also:
Adultery
Communication
Divorce
Marriage
Marriage Guidance
Sex, Normal
Wives

He who finds a wife finds what is good and receives favor from the LORD.
(Proverbs 18:22)

Husbands, love your wives, just as Christ loved the church and gave himself up for her to make her holy.
(Ephesians 5:25-26)

For the husband is the head of the wife as Christ is the head of the church, his body, of which he is the Savior.
(Ephesians 5:23)

Husbands, in the same way be considerate as you live with your wives, and treat them with respect as the weaker partner and as heirs with you of the gracious gift of life, so that nothing will hinder your prayers.
(1 Peter 3:7)

Husbands, love your wives and do not be harsh with them.
(Colossians 3:19)

Each one of you also must love his wife as he loves himself, and the wife must respect her husband.
(Ephesians 5:33)

Husbands ought to love their wives as their own bodies. He who loves his wife loves himself.
(Ephesians 5:28)

After all, no one ever hated his own body, but he feeds and cares for it, just as Christ does the church.
(Ephesians 5:29)

Under three things the earth trembles, under four it
cannot bear up: a servant who becomes king, a fool who
is full of food, an unloved woman who is married, and a
maidservant who displaces her mistress.
(Proverbs 30:21-23)

Your wife will be like a fruitful vine within your house;
your sons will be like olive shoots around your table.
Thus is the man blessed who fears the LORD.
(Psalm 128:3-4)

HYPOCRITICAL

See also:
God, All Knowing
God, Present
   Everywhere
Sinful Nature

*Woe to you, teachers of the law and
Pharisees, you hypocrites! You clean
the outside of the cup and dish, but
inside they are full of greed and
self-indulgence.*
(Matthew 23:25)

*First clean the inside of the cup and dish, and then the outside
also will be clean.*
(Matthew 23:26)

*Woe to you, teachers of the law and Pharisees, you hypocrites!
You are like whitewashed tombs, which look beautiful on the
outside but on the inside are full of dead man's bones and
everything unclean.*
(Matthew 23:27)

*On the outside you appear to people as righteous but on the
inside you are full of hypocrisy and wickedness.*
(Matthew 23:28)

*These people honor me with their lips, but their hearts are far
from me. They worship me in vain; their teachings are but
rules taught by men.*
(Mark 7:6-7)

*You have let go of the commands of God and are holding on to
the traditions of men.*
(Mark 7:8)

*The teachers of the law and the Pharisees sit in Moses' seat. So
you must obey them and do everything they tell you. But do
not do what they do, for they do not practice what they preach.*
(Matthew 23:2-3)

Woe to you Pharisees, because you give God a tenth of your mint, rue and all other kinds of garden herbs, but you neglect justice and the love of God. You should have practiced the latter without leaving the former undone.
(Luke 11:42)

And you experts in the law, woe to you, because you load people down with burdens they can hardly carry, and you yourselves will not lift one finger to help them.
(Luke 11:46)

Woe to you experts in the law, because you have taken away the key to knowledge. You yourselves have not entered, and you have hindered those who were entering.
(Luke 11:52)

Beware of the teachers of the law. They like to walk around in flowing robes and love to be greeted in the marketplaces and have the most important seats in the synagogues and the places of honor at banquets. They devour widows' houses and for a show make lengthy prayers. Such men will be punished most severely.
(Luke 20:46-47)

IMPATIENT

See also:
Anger
Friendship
Holy Spirit
Love, For Others
Peace

Be patient, bearing with one
another in love.
(Ephesians 4:2)

Love is patient, love is kind. It does not envy, it does not
boast, it is not proud.
(1 Corinthians 13:4)

A patient man has great understanding, but a
quick-tempered man displays folly.
(Proverbs 14:29)

It is not good to have zeal without knowledge, nor to be
hasty and miss the way.
(Proverbs 19:2)

A man's wisdom gives him patience; it is to his glory to
overlook an offense.
(Proverbs 19:11)

Better a patient man than a warrior, a man who controls
his temper than one who takes a city.
(Proverbs 16:32)

A hot-tempered man stirs up dissension, but a patient
man calms a quarrel.
(Proverbs 15:18)

Be joyful in hope, patient in affliction, faithful in prayer.
(Romans 12:12)

And we urge you, brothers, warn those who are idle, encourage the timid, help the weak, be patient with everyone.
(1 Thessalonians 5:14)

INTELLIGENCE

See also:
Boastful
Conceit
God, All Knowing
Humility
Pride
Wisdom

Where is the wise man? Where is the scholar? Where is the philosopher of this age? Has not God made foolish the wisdom of the world?
(1 Corinthians 1:20)

Do not deceive yourselves. If any one of you thinks he is wise by the standards of this age, he should become a "fool" so that he may become wise.
(1 Corinthians 3:18)

The man who thinks he knows something does not yet know as he ought to know.
(1 Corinthians 8:2)

Woe to those who are wise in their own eyes and clever in their own sight.
(Isaiah 5:21)

The Lord knows that the thoughts of the wise are futile.
(1 Corinthians 3:20)

The wisdom of the wise will perish, the intelligence of the intelligent will vanish.
(Isaiah 29:14)

For the foolishness of God is wiser than man's wisdom, and the weakness of God is stronger than man's strength.
(1 Corinthians 1:25)

Knowledge puffs up, but love builds up.
(1 Corinthians 8:1)

The arrogant cannot stand in your presence.
(Psalm 5:5)

I hate pride and arrogance, evil behavior and perverse speech.
(Proverbs 8:13)

Since they have rejected the word of the LORD, what kind of wisdom do they have?
(Jeremiah 8:9)

Arrogant lips are unsuited to a fool.
(Proverbs 17:7)

I will destroy the wisdom of the wise; the intelligence of the intelligent I will frustrate.
(1 Corinthians 1:19)

Not many of you were wise by human standards; not many were influential; not many were of noble birth.
(1 Corinthians 1:26)

But God chose the foolish things of the world to shame the wise.
(1 Corinthians 1:27)

My message and my preaching were not with wise and persuasive words, but with a demonstration of the Spirit's power, so that your faith might not rest on men's wisdom, but on God's power.
(1 Corinthians 2:4-5)

For the wisdom of this world is foolishness in God's sight.
(1 Corinthians 3:19)

The eyes of the arrogant man will be humbled and the pride of men brought low.
(Isaiah 2:11)

Do you see a man wise in his own eyes? There is more hope for a fool than for him.
(Proverbs 26:12)

JOY

See also:
Blessings
Holy Spirit
Praise Him
Sing Praises
Thankful
Worship

This is the day the LORD has made;
let us rejoice and be glad in it.
(Psalm 118:24)

Shout for joy to the LORD, all the earth,
burst into jubilant song with music.
(Psalm 98:4)

Let the heavens rejoice, let the earth be glad; let the sea
resound, and all that is in it; let the fields be jubilant, and
everything in them.
(Psalm 96:11-12)

Let the rivers clap their hands, let the mountains sing
together for joy.
(Psalm 98:8)

Clap your hands, all you nations; shout to God with cries
of joy.
(Psalm 47:1)

I delight greatly in the LORD; my soul rejoices in my God.
(Isaiah 61:10)

My heart leaps for joy and I will give thanks to Him in
song.
(Psalm 28:7)

My lips will shout for joy when I sing praise to you — I,
whom you have redeemed.
(Psalm 71:23)

For you make me glad by your deeds, O LORD; I sing for
joy at the works of your hands.
(Psalm 92:4)

Let the righteous rejoice in the LORD and take refuge in him; let all the upright in heart praise him!
(Psalm 64:10)

Shout for joy to the LORD, all the earth.
(Psalm 100:1)

Rejoice in the Lord always. I will say it again: Rejoice!
(Philippians 4:4)

Bring joy to your servant, for to you, O Lord, I lift up my soul.
(Psalm 86:4)

You will fill me with joy in your presence, with eternal pleasures at your right hand.
(Psalm 16:11)

The precepts of the LORD are right, giving joy to the heart.
(Psalm 19:8)

I have told you this so that my joy may be in you and that your joy may be complete.
(John 15:11)

I am coming to you now, but I say these things while I am still in the world, so that they may have the full measure of my joy within them.
(John 17:13)

Be joyful in hope, patient in affliction, faithful in prayer.
(Romans 12:12)

Hallelujah! For our Lord God Almighty reigns. Let us rejoice and be glad and give him glory!
(Revelation 19:6-7)

JUDGMENTAL

See also:
Anger
Forgive
Hatred
Love, For Others
Vengeance

*Do not judge, and you will not be judged.
Do not condemn, and you will not be
condemned.*
(Luke 6:37)

*For in the same way you judge others, you will be judged, and
with the measure you use, it will be measured to you.*
(Matthew 7:2)

*Why do you look at the speck of sawdust in your brother's eye
and pay no attention to the plank in your own eye? How can
you say to your brother, "Let me take the speck out of your
eye," when all the time there is a plank in your own eye?*
(Matthew 7:3-4)

*You hypocrite, first take the plank out of your own eye, and then
you will see clearly to remove the speck from your brother's eye.*
(Matthew 7:5)

For at whatever point you judge the other, you are con-
demning yourself, because you who pass judgment do
the same things.
(Romans 2:1)

Anyone who speaks against his brother or judges him
speaks against the law and judges it. When you judge the
law, you are not keeping it, but sitting judgment on it.
(James 4:11)

There is only one Lawgiver and Judge, the one who is able to
save and destroy. But you — who are you to judge your
neighbor?
(James 4:12)

So when you, a mere man, pass judgment on them and yet do the same things, do you think you will escape God's judgment?
(Romans 2:3)

You judge by human standards; I pass judgement on no one. But if I do judge, my decisions are right, because I am not alone. I stand with the Father, who sent me.
(John 8:15-16)

And will not God bring about justice for his chosen ones, who cry out to him day and night? Will he keep putting them off? I tell you, he will see that they get justice, and quickly.
(Luke 18:7-8)

You, then, why do you judge your brother? Or why do you look down on your brother? For we will all stand before God's judgment seat.
(Romans 14:10)

Each of us will give an account of himself to God. Therefore let us stop passing judgment on one another.
(Romans 14:12-13)

Accept him whose faith is weak, without passing judgment on disputable matters.
(Romans 14:1)

The spiritual man makes judgments about all things, but he himself is not subject to any man's judgment.
(1 Corinthians 2:15)

I do not even judge myself. My conscience is clear, but that does not make me innocent.
(1 Corinthians 4:3-4)

It is the Lord who judges me. Therefore judge nothing before the appointed time; wait till the Lord comes.
(1 Corinthians 4:4-5)

LAZINESS

See also:
Occupation/Job/Work

In the name of the Lord Jesus Christ, we command you, brothers, to keep away from every brother who is idle and who does not live according to the teaching you received from us.
(2 Thessalonians 3:6)

If a man is lazy, the rafters sag; if his hands are idle, the house leaks.
(Ecclesiastes 10:18)

Lazy hands make a man poor, but diligent hands bring wealth.
(Proverbs 10:4)

The fool folds his hands and ruins himself.
(Ecclesiastes 4:5)

Diligent hands will rule, but laziness ends in slave labor.
(Proverbs 12:24)

If a man will not work, he shall not eat.
(2 Thessalonians 3:10)

A sluggard does not plow in season; so at harvest time he looks but finds nothing.
(Proverbs 20:4)

Go to the ant, you sluggard; consider its ways and be wise! It has no commander, no overseer or ruler, yet it stores its provisions in summer and gathers its food at harvest.
(Proverbs 6:6-8)

As vinegar to the teeth and smoke to the eyes, so is a sluggard to those who send him.
(Proverbs 10:26)

The sluggard craves and gets nothing, but the desires of the diligent are fully satisfied.
(Proverbs 13:4)

How long will you lie there, you sluggard? When will you get up from your sleep? A little sleep, a little slumber, a little folding of the hands to rest — and poverty will come on you like a bandit and scarcity like an armed man.
(Proverbs 6:9-11)

Laziness brings on deep sleep, and the shiftless man goes hungry.
(Proverbs 19:15)

Do not love sleep or you will grow poor; stay awake and you will have food to spare.
(Proverbs 20:13)

A little sleep, a little slumber, a little folding of the hands to rest — and poverty will come on you like a bandit and scarcity like an armed man.
(Proverbs 24:33-34)

As a door turns on its hinges, so a sluggard turns on his bed.
(Proverbs 26:14)

We do not want you to become lazy, but to imitate those who through faith and patience inherit what has been promised.
(Hebrews 6:12)

LIGHT

See also:
Christ, Identity Of
Darkness
Righteous
Truth

God is light; in him there is no
darkness at all.
(1 John 1:5)

Let the light of your face shine upon us, O Lord.
(Psalm 4:6)

For with you is the fountain of life; in your light we see
light.
(Psalm 36:9)

The Lord is God, and he has made his light shine upon
us.
(Psalm 118:27)

For God, who said, "Let light shine out of darkness,"
made his light shine in our hearts to give us the light of
the knowledge of the glory of God in the face of Christ.
(2 Corinthians 4:6)

In him was life, and that life was the light of men.
(John 1:4)

While I am in the world, I am the light of the world.
(John 9:5)

*You are going to have the light just a little while longer. Walk
while you have the light, before darkness overtakes you.*
(John 12:35)

*Put your trust in the light while you have it, so that you may
become sons of light.*
(John 12:36)

If we claim to have fellowship with him yet walk in the darkness, we lie and do not live by the truth.
(1 John 1:6)

But if we walk in the light as he is in the light, we have fellowship with one another, and the blood of Jesus, his Son, purifies us from all sin.
(1 John 1:7)

No one lights a lamp and puts it in a place where it will be hidden, or under a bowl. Instead he puts it on its stand, so that those who come in may see the light.
(Luke 11:33)

Therefore, if your whole body is full of light, and no part of it dark, it will be completely lighted, as when the light of a lamp shines on you.
(Luke 11:36)

Light is shed upon the righteous and joy on the upright in heart.
(Psalm 97:11)

I was blind but now I see!
(John 9:25)

Live as children of light.
(Ephesians 5:8)

LONELINESS

See also:
God, All Loving
God, Present Everywhere
Help
Grief
Guidance
Love, By God
Refuge/Safety

The Lord is near.
(Philippians 4:5)

The LORD is near to all who call on him, to all who call on him in truth.
(Psalm 145:18)

For none of us lives to himself alone and none of us dies to himself alone.
(Romans 14:7)

He is not far from each one of us.
(Acts 17:27)

Come near to God and he will come near to you.
(James 4:8)

Turn to me and be gracious to me, for I am lonely and afflicted.
(Psalm 25:16)

Be not far from me, O God; come quickly, O my God, to help me.
(Psalm 71:12)

And I will ask the Father, and he will give you another Counselor to be with you forever — the Spirit of truth.
(John 14:16-17)

I will not leave you as orphans; I will come to you.
(John 14:18)

God sets the lonely in families.
(Psalm 68:6)

Yet I am not alone, for my Father is with me.
(John 16:32)

As the mountains surround Jerusalem, so the LORD surrounds his people both now and forevermore.
(Psalm 125:2)

The LORD Almighty is with us.
(Psalm 46:11)

Yet you are near, O LORD, and all your commands are true.
(Psalm 119:151)

And surely I am with you always, to the very end of the age.
(Matthew 28:20)

LORD'S PRAYER

> **See also:**
> Prayer, How To

This, then, is how you should pray:

> *"Our Father in heaven,*
> *hallowed be your name,*
> *your kingdom come,*
> *your will be done*
> *on earth as it is in heaven.*
> *Give us today our daily bread.*
> *Forgive us our debts,*
> *as we also have forgiven our debtors.*
> *And lead us not into temptation,*
> *but deliver us from the evil one."*
> **(Matthew 6:9-13)**

LOVE, BY GOD

| See also:
| God, All Loving

For God so loved the world that he gave his one and only Son, that whoever believes in him shall not perish but have eternal life.
(John 3:16)

This is how God showed his love among us: He sent his one and only Son into the world that we might live through him.
(1 John 4:9)

This is love: not that we loved God, but that he loved us and sent his Son as an atoning sacrifice for our sins.
(1 John 4:10)

We love because he first loved us.
(1 John 4:19)

For Christ's love compels us, because we are convinced that one died for all, and therefore all died.
(2 Corinthians 5:14)

As the Father has loved me, so have I loved you. Now remain in my love.
(John 15:9)

The Father himself loves you because you have loved me and have believed that I came from God.
(John 16:27)

I have made you known to them, and will continue to make you known in order that the love you have for me may be in them and that I myself may be in them.
(John 17:26)

And I pray that you, being rooted and established in love, may have power, together with all the saints, to grasp how wide and long and high and deep is the love of Christ, and to know this love that surpasses knowledge — that you may be filled to the measure of all the fullness of God.
(Ephesians 3:17-19)

May the Lord direct your hearts into God's love and Christ's perseverance.
(2 Thessalonians 3:5)

Keep yourselves in God's love as you wait for the mercy of our Lord Jesus Christ to bring you to eternal life.
(Jude 1:21)

LOVE, FOR CHRIST

See also:
Action
Commandments
Disobedience
Obedience

If you love me, you will obey what I command.
(John 14:15)

Whoever has my commands and obeys them, he is the one who loves me.
(John 14:21)

He who loves me will be loved by my Father, and I too will love him and show myself to him.
(John 14:21)

If anyone loves me, he will obey my teaching. My Father will love him, and we will come to him and make our home with him.
(John 14:23)

He who does not love me will not obey my teaching.
(John 14:24)

Anyone who loves his father or mother more than me is not worthy of me; anyone who loves his son or daughter more than me is not worthy of me; and anyone who does not take his cross and follow me is not worthy of me.
(Matthew 10:37-38)

Grace to all who love our Lord Jesus Christ with an undying love.
(Ephesians 6:24)

Though you have not seen him, you love him; and even though you do not see him now, you believe in him and are filled with an inexpressible and glorious joy.
(1 Peter 1:8)

LOVE, FOR GOD

See also:
Love, By God
Love, For Others

Love the Lord God with all your heart and
with all your soul and with all your mind.
This is the first and greatest commandment.
(Matthew 22:37-38)

Love the LORD your God and keep his requirements, his
decrees, his laws and his commands always.
(Deuteronomy 11:1)

The man who loves God is known by God.
(1 Corinthians 8:3)

I love those who love me, and those who seek me find me.
(Proverbs 8:17)

"Because he loves me," says the LORD, "I will rescue him;
I will protect him, for he acknowledges my name."
(Psalm 91:14)

The LORD watches over all who love him, but all the
wicked he will destroy.
(Psalm 145:20)

So be very careful to love the LORD your God.
(Joshua 23:11)

Love the LORD, all his saints!
(Psalm 31:23)

Delight yourself in the LORD and he will give you the
desires of your heart.
(Psalm 37:4)

Whom have I in heaven but you? And earth has nothing I desire besides you.
(Psalm 73:25)

My flesh and my heart may fail, but God is the strength of my heart and my portion forever.
(Psalm 73:26)

And we know that in all things God works for the good of those who love him, who have been called according to his purpose.
(Romans 8:28)

I love you, O LORD, my strength.
(Psalm 18:1)

LOVE, FOR OTHERS

See also:
Church
Friendship
Holy Spirit
Love, By God
Love, General

Dear friends, let us love another,
for love comes from God.
(1 John 4:7)

Dear friends, since God so loved us, we also ought to
love one another.
(1 John 4:11)

My command is this: Love each other as I have loved you.
(John 15:12)

Love one another deeply, from the heart.
(1 Peter 1:22)

Be devoted to one another in brotherly love.
(Romans 12:10)

Love your neighbor as yourself.
(Mark 12:31)

Whoever loves his brother lives in the light, and there is
nothing in him to make him stumble.
(1 John 2:10)

No one has ever seen God; but if we love one another,
God lives in us and his love is made complete in us.
(1 John 4:12)

Remember those in prison as if you were their fellow
prisoners, and those who are mistreated as if you yourselves were suffering.
(Hebrews 13:3)

*If you love those who love you, what reward will you get? Are
not even the tax collectors doing that?*
(Matthew 5:46)

This is how we know what love is: Jesus Christ laid down his life for us. And we ought to lay down our lives for our brothers.
(1 John 3:16)

Greater love has no one than this, that he lay down his life for his friends.
(John 15:13)

Keep on loving each other as brothers.
(Hebrews 13:1)

Above all, love each other deeply, because love covers over a multitude of sins.
(1 Peter 4:8)

By this all men will know that you are my disciples, if you love one another.
(John 13:35)

May the Lord make your love increase and overflow for each other and for everyone else, just as ours does for you.
(1 Thessalonians 3:12)

Let no debt remain outstanding, except the continuing debt to love one another, for he who loves his fellow man has fulfilled the law.
(Romans 13:8)

So in everything, do to others what you would have them do to you, for this sums up the Law and the Prophets.
(Matthew 7:12)

LOVE, GENERAL

See also:
Love, For Others

If I speak in the tongues of men and of angels, but have not love, I am only a resounding gong or a clanging cymbal.
(1 Corinthians 13:1)

If I have the gift of prophecy and can fathom all mysteries and all knowledge, and if I have a faith that can move mountains, but have not love, I am nothing.
(1 Corinthians 13:2)

If I give all I possess to the poor and surrender my body to the flames, but have not love, I gain nothing.
(1 Corinthians 13:3)

Love is patient, love is kind. It does not envy, it does not boast, it is not proud. It is not rude, it is not self-seeking, it is not easily angered, it keeps no record of wrongs.
(1 Corinthians 13:4-5)

Love does not delight in evil but rejoices with the truth. It always protects, always trusts, always hopes, always preserves.
(1 Corinthians 13:6-7)

Love never fails.
(1 Corinthians 13:8)

And now these three remain: faith, hope and love. But the greatest of these is love.
(1 Corinthians 13:13)

Do everything in love.
(1 Corinthians 16:14)

Be imitators of God, therefore, as dearly loved children and live a life of love, just as Christ loved us and gave himself up for us as a fragrant offering and sacrifice to God.
(Ephesians 5:1-2)

Anyone who does not love remains in death.
(1 John 3:14)

Everyone who loves has been born of God and knows God.
(1 John 4:7)

As you heard from the beginning, his command is that you walk in love.
(2 John 1:6)

The goal of this command is love, which comes from a pure heart and a good conscience and a sincere faith.
(1 Timothy 1:5)

The only thing that counts is faith expressing itself through love.
(Galatians 5:6)

Love must be sincere.
(Romans 12:9)

Let love and faithfulness never leave you; bind them around your neck, write them on the tablet of your heart.
(Proverbs 3:3)

LUST

See also:
Adultery
Homosexuality
Promiscuity
Prostitution
Sex, Perverted

I made a covenant with my eyes
not to look lustfully at a girl.
(Job 31:1)

Those who belong to Christ Jesus have crucified the
sinful nature with its passions and desires.
(Galatians 5:24)

For you have spent enough time in the past doing what
pagans choose to do — living in debauchery, lust, drunkenness, orgies, carousing and detestable idolatry.
(1 Peter 4:3)

It is God's will that you should be sanctified: that you
should avoid sexual immorality; that each of you should
learn to control his own body in a way that is holy and
honorable, not in passionate lust like the heathen, who
do not know God; and that in this matter no one should
wrong his brother or take advantage of him.
(1 Thessalonians 4:3-5)

Treat younger men as brothers, older women as mothers,
and younger women as sisters, with absolute purity.
(1 Timothy 5:1-2)

Let us be self-controlled, putting on faith and love as a
breastplate, and hope of salvation as a helmet.
(1 Thessalonians 5:8)

Encourage the young men to be self-controlled.
(Titus 2:6)

Flee the evil desires of youth, and pursue righteousness, faith, love and peace, along with those who call on the Lord out of a pure heart.
(2 Timothy 2:22)

You have heard that it was said, "Do not commit adultery." But I tell you that anyone who looks at a woman lustfully has already committed adultery with her in his heart.
(Matthew 5:27-28)

Like a city whose walls are broken down is a man who lacks self-control.
(Proverbs 25:28)

Therefore do not let sin reign in your mortal body so that you obey its evil desires.
(Romans 6:12)

LYING

See also:
Communication
Dishonesty
Slander
Truth

Do not lie. Do not deceive one
another.
(Leviticus 19:11)

No one who practices deceit will dwell in my house; no
one who speaks falsely will stand in my presence.
(Psalm 101:7)

The LORD detests lying lips, but he delights in men who
are truthful.
(Proverbs 12:22)

You destroy those who tell lies; bloodthirsty and deceitful men the LORD abhors.
(Psalm 5:6)

Better to be poor than a liar.
(Proverbs 19:22)

He whose tongue is deceitful falls into trouble.
(Proverbs 17:20)

O Lord, do not your eyes look for truth?
(Jeremiah 5:3)

Truthful lips endure forever, but a lying tongue lasts only
a moment.
(Proverbs 12:19)

An honest answer is like a kiss on the lips.
(Proverbs 24:26)

The righteous hate what is false, but the wicked bring
shame and disgrace.
(Proverbs 13:5)

The integrity of the upright guides them, but the unfaithful are destroyed by their duplicity.
(Proverbs 11:3)

I hate and abhor falsehood but I love your law.
(Psalm 119:163)

A lying tongue hates those it hurts, and a flattering mouth works ruin.
(Proverbs 26:28)

Friend deceives friend, and no one speaks the truth. They have taught their tongues to lie; they weary themselves with sinning.
(Jeremiah 9:5)

You love evil rather than good, falsehood rather than speaking the truth.
(Psalm 52:3)

Like a club or a sword or a sharp arrow is the man who gives false testimony against his neighbor.
(Proverbs 25:18)

Like a madman shooting firebrands or deadly arrows is a man who deceives his neighbor and says, "I was only joking!"
(Proverbs 26:18-19)

Therefore each of you must put off falsehood and speak truthfully to his neighbor, for we are all members of one body.
(Ephesians 4:25)

You shall not give false testimony against your neighbor.
(Deuteronomy 5:20)

Keep falsehood and lies far from me.
(Proverbs 30:7-8)

Keep me from deceitful ways; be gracious to me through
your law.
(Psalm 119:29)

Whoever of you loves life and desires to see many good
days, keep your tongue from evil and your lips from
speaking lies.
(Psalm 34:12-13)

*For by your words you will be acquitted, and by your words
you will be condemned.*
(Matthew 12:37)

MARRIAGE

See also:
Communication
Divorce
Husbands
Marriage Guidance
Sex, Normal
Wives

*But at the beginning of creation God
"made them male and female."*
(Mark 10:6)

*For this reason a man will leave his
father and mother and be united to his
wife, and the two will become one flesh.*
(Mark 10:7-8)

*So they are no longer two, but one. Therefore, what God has
joined together, let man not separate.*
(Mark 10:8-9)

The disciples said to him, "If this is the situation between a
husband and wife, it is better not to marry." Jesus replied,
*Not everyone can accept this word, but only those to whom it has
been given.*
(Matthew 19:10-11)

*For some are eunuchs because they were born that way; others
were made that way by men; and others have renounced marriage because of the kingdom of heaven. The one who can accept
this should accept it.*
(Matthew 19:12)

It is good for man not to marry. But since there is so
much immorality, each man should have his own wife,
and each woman her own husband.
(1 Corinthians 7:1-2)

So I counsel younger widows to marry, to have children,
to manage their homes and to give the enemy no opportunity for slander.
(1 Timothy 5:14)

Now to the unmarried and the widows I say: It is good for them to stay unmarried, as I am. But if they cannot control themselves, they should marry, for it is better to marry than to burn with passion.
(1 Corinthians 7:8-9)

A woman is bound to her husband as long as he lives. But if her husband dies, she is free to marry anyone she wishes, but he must belong to the Lord.
(1 Corinthians 7:39)

Do not be yoked together with unbelievers. For what do righteousness and wickedness have in common? Or what fellowship can light have with darkness?
(2 Corinthians 6:14)

But those who are considered worthy of taking part in that age and in the resurrection will neither marry nor be given in marriage, and they can no longer die; for they are like the angels.
(Luke 20:35-36)

When the dead rise, they will neither marry nor be given in marriage; they will be like the angels in heaven.
(Mark 12:25)

MARRIAGE GUIDANCE

See also:
Adultery
Argumentative
Communication
Divorce
Husbands
Marriage
Sex, Normal
Wives

A gentle answer turns away wrath,
but a harsh word stirs up anger.
(Proverbs 15:1)

Pleasant words are a honeycomb, sweet to the soul and
healing to the bones.
(Proverbs 16:24)

A man finds joy in giving an apt reply — and how good
is a timely word!
(Proverbs 15:23)

A word aptly spoken is like apples of gold in settings of
silver.
(Proverbs 25:11)

When words are many, sin is not absent, but he who
holds his tongue is wise.
(Proverbs 10:19)

He who answers before listening — that is his folly and
his shame.
(Proverbs 18:13)

A fool shows his annoyance at once, but a prudent man
overlooks an insult.
(Proverbs 12:16)

Do not pay attention to every word people say.
(Ecclesiastes 7:21)

Starting a quarrel is like breaching a dam; so drop the matter before a dispute breaks out.
(Proverbs 17:14)

As charcoal to embers and as wood to fire, so is a quarrelsome man for kindling strife.
(Proverbs 26:21)

A quarrelsome wife is like a constant dripping.
(Proverbs 19:13)

Better to live in a corner of the roof than share a house with a quarrelsome wife.
(Proverbs 21:9)

Better to live in a desert than with a quarrelsome and ill-tempered wife.
(Proverbs 21:19)

A quarrelsome wife is like a constant dripping on a rainy day; restraining her is like restraining the wind or grasping oil with the hand.
(Proverbs 27:15-16)

He who loves a quarrel loves sin; he who builds a high gate invites destruction.
(Proverbs 17:19)

An offended brother is more unyielding than a fortified city, and disputes are like the barred gates of a citadel.
(Proverbs 18:19)

Better a dry crust with peace and quiet than a house full of feasting, with strife.
(Proverbs 17:1)

Let your gentleness be evident to all.
(Philippians 4:5)

It is to a man's honor to avoid strife.
(Proverbs 20:3)

A cheerful look brings joy to the heart, and good news gives health to the bones.
(Proverbs 15:30)

So in everything, do to others what you would have them do to you.
(Matthew 7:12)

A gift given in secret soothes anger.
(Proverbs 21:14)

MEDITATION

See also:
Prayer, How To
Scripture/Word

I will meditate on all your mighty works
and consider all your mighty deeds.
(Psalm 77:12)

I meditate on all your works and consider what your
hands have done.
(Psalm 143:5)

Within your temple, O God, we meditate on your unfailing love.
(Psalm 48:9)

May my meditation be pleasing to him, as I rejoice in the LORD.
(Psalm 104:34)

Oh, how I love your law! I meditate on it all day long.
Your commands make me wiser than my enemies, for
they are ever with me.
(Psalm 119:97-98)

I have more insight than all my teachers, for I meditate
on your statutes.
(Psalm 119:99)

I meditate on your precepts and consider your ways.
(Psalm 119:15)

I lift up my hands to your commands, which I love, and I
meditate on your decrees.
(Psalm 119:48)

Do not let this Book of the Law depart from your mouth; meditate on it day and night, so that you may be careful to do everything written in it. Then you will be prosperous and successful.
(Joshua 1:8)

MERCY

See also:
Blessings
Forgiveness
Help
Hopeless
Prayer, Answers To
Protection
Refuge/Safety

O LORD, hear my prayer, listen to my cry for mercy; in your faithfulness and righteousness come to my relief.
(Psalm 143:1)

Hear my cry for mercy as I call to you for help, as I lift up my hands toward your Most Holy Place.
(Psalm 28:2)

Hear, O LORD, and be merciful to me; O LORD, be my help.
(Psalm 30:10)

Do not withhold your mercy from me, O LORD.
(Psalm 40:11)

The Lord our God is merciful and forgiving, even though we have rebelled against him.
(Daniel 9:9)

The LORD has heard my cry for mercy; the LORD accepts my prayer.
(Psalm 6:9)

Blessed are the merciful, for they will be shown mercy.
(Matthew 5:7)

Be merciful, just as your Father is merciful.
(Luke 6:36)

Because of his great love for us, God, who is rich in mercy, made us alive with Christ even when we were dead in transgressions — it is by grace you have been saved.
(Ephesians 2:4-5)

And what does the LORD require of you? To act justly and to love mercy and to walk humbly with your God.
(Micah 6:8)

MONEY

See also:
Envy/Jealous
Giving
Greedy/Stingy
Poverty
Riches, Beware Of
Riches, True
Self-Sacrifice
Worldly

Keep your lives free from the love of money and be content with what you have, because God has said, "Never will I leave you; never will I forsake you."
(Hebrews 13:5)

Some people, eager for money, have wandered from the faith and pierced themselves with many griefs.
(1 Timothy 6:10)

People who want to get rich fall into temptation and a trap and into many foolish and harmful desires that plunge men into ruin and destruction.
(1 Timothy 6:9)

For the love of money is a root of all kinds of evil.
(1 Timothy 6:10)

The wealth of the rich is their fortified city; they imagine it an unscalable wall.
(Proverbs 18:11)

You say, "I am rich; I have acquired wealth and do not need a thing." But you do not realize that you are wretched, pitiful, poor, blind and naked.
(Revelation 3:17)

Whoever loves money never has money enough; whoever loves wealth is never satisfied with his income. This too is meaningless.
(Ecclesiastes 5:10)

Man is a mere phantom as he goes to and fro: He bustles about, but only in vain; he heaps up wealth, not knowing who will get it.
(Psalm 39:6)

For the sun rises with scorching heat and withers the plant; its blossom falls and its beauty is destroyed. In the same way, the rich man will fade away even while he goes about his business.
(James 1:11)

How hard it is for the rich to enter the kingdom of God!
(Mark 10:23)

It is easier for a camel to go through the eye of a needle than for a rich man to enter the kingdom of God.
(Mark 10:25)

Now listen, you rich people, weep and wail because of the misery that is coming upon you...You have lived on earth in luxury and self-indulgence.
(James 5:1-5)

No servant can serve two masters. Either he will hate the one and love the other, or he will be devoted to the one and despise the other. You cannot serve both God and Money.
(Luke 16:13)

MORTAL MAN

See also:
Death/Dying
Eternal Life
God, Eternal
Heaven
Salvation

Each man's life is but a breath.
(Psalm 39:5)

All men are like grass, and all their glory is like the flowers of the field; the grass withers and the flowers fall, but the word of the Lord stands forever.
(1 Peter 1:24-25)

Stop trusting in man who has but a breath in his nostrils. Of what account is he?
(Isaiah 2:22)

For we were born only yesterday and know nothing, and our days on earth are but a shadow.
(Job 8:9)

You have made my day as a mere hand breath; the span of my years is as nothing before you.
(Psalm 39:5)

You consume their wealth like a moth — each man is but a breath.
(Psalm 39:11)

What is your life? You are a mist that appears for a little while and then vanishes.
(James 4:14)

Man is like a breath; his days are like a fleeting shadow.
(Psalm 144:4)

As for man, his days are like grass, he flourishes like a flower of the field; the wind blows over it and it is gone, and its place remembers it no more.
(Psalm 103:15-16)

The length of our days is seventy years — or eighty, if we have the strength; yet their span is but trouble and sorrow, for they quickly pass, and we fly away.
(Psalm 90:10)

Teach us to number our days aright, that we may gain a heart of wisdom.
(Psalm 90:12)

OBEDIENCE

See also:
Action
Disobedience
Love, For Christ
Righteous
Truth

Obey me and do everything I command you, and you will be my people, and I will be your God.
(Jeremiah 11:4)

If you love me, you will obey what I command.
(John 14:15)

If you obey my commands, you will remain in my love, just as I have obeyed my Father's commands and remain in his love.
(John 15:10)

This is how we know we are in him: Whoever claims to live in him must walk as Jesus did.
(1 John 2:5-6)

We know that we have come to know him if we obey his commands.
(1 John 2:3)

Those who obey his commands live in him, and he in them.
(1 John 3:24)

This is how we know that we love the children of God: by loving God and carrying out his commands.
(1 John 5:2)

This is love for God: to obey his commands.
(1 John 5:3)

And his commands are not burdensome, for everyone born of God overcomes the world.
(1 John 5:3-4)

Anyone who listens to the word but does not do what it
says is like a man who looks at his face in a mirror and,
after looking at himself, goes away and immediately
forgets what he looks like. But the man who looks in-
tently into the perfect law that gives freedom, and continues to do this, not forgetting what he has heard, but
doing it — he will be blessed in what he does.
(James 1:23-25)

If you are willing and obedient, you will eat the best from
the land.
(Isaiah 1:19)

Blessed are they whose ways are blameless, who walk
according to the law of the LORD.
(Psalm 119:1)

I obey your statutes, for I love them greatly.
(Psalm 119:167)

Wait for the LORD and keep his way.
(Psalm 37:34)

OCCULT

See also:
Devil
Evil, Resisting

Do not practice divination or sorcery.
(Leviticus 19:26)

Let no one be found among you who sacrifices his son or
daughter in the fire, who practices divination or sorcery,
interprets omens, engages in witchcraft, or casts spells, or
who is a medium or spiritist or who consults the dead.
Anyone who does these things is detestable to the LORD.
(Deuteronomy 18:10-12)

When men tell you to consult mediums and spiritists,
who whisper and mutter, should not a people inquire of
their God? Why consult the dead on behalf of the living?
(Isaiah 8:19)

Do not turn to mediums or seek out spiritists, for you
will be defiled by them. I am the LORD your God.
(Leviticus 19:31)

I will set my face against the person who turns to mediums and spiritists to prostitute himself by following
them, and I will cut him off from his people.
(Leviticus 20:6)

Have nothing to do with godless myths and old wives'
tales; rather, train yourselves to be godly.
(1 Timothy 4:7)

Command certain men not to teach false doctrines any
longer nor to devote themselves to myths and endless
genealogies. These promote controversies rather than
God's work — which is by faith.
(1 Timothy 1:3-4)

No wise man, enchanter, magician or diviner can explain
to the king the mystery he has asked about, but there is a
God in heaven who reveals mysteries.
(Daniel 2:27-28)

Let your astrologers come forward, those stargazers who
make predictions month by month, let them save you
from what is coming upon you.
(Isaiah 47:13)

Keep on, then, with your magic spells and with your
many sorceries, which you have labored at since child-
hood. Perhaps you will succeed, perhaps you will cause
terror. All the counsel you have received has only worn
you out!
(Isaiah 47:12-13)

I will destroy your witchcraft and you will no longer cast
spells.
 Micah 5:12)

They did not stop worshiping demons, and idols of gold,
silver, bronze, stone and wood — idols that cannot see or
hear or walk. Nor did they repent of their murders, their
magic arts, their sexual immorality or their thefts.
(Revelation 9:20-21)

Outside are the dogs, those who practice magic arts, the
sexually immoral, the murderers, the idolaters and everyone who loves and practices falsehood.
(Revelation 22:15)

OCCUPATION/ JOB/WORK

See also:
Laziness
Plans
Self-Sacrifice
Servant
Will of God

Whatever you do, work at it with all your heart, as working for the Lord, not for men, since you know that you will receive an inheritance from the Lord as a reward.
(Colossians 3:23-24)

Brothers, each man, as responsible to God, should remain in the situation God called him to.
(1 Corinthians 7:24)

There are different kinds of service, but the same Lord.
(1 Corinthians 12:5)

There are different kinds of working, but the same God works all of them in all men.
(1 Corinthians 12:6)

Therefore I glory in Christ Jesus in my service to God.
(Romans 15:17)

Each one should test his own actions. Then he can take pride in himself, without comparing himself to somebody else, for each one should carry his own load.
(Galatians 6:4-5)

Do not wear yourself out to get rich; have the wisdom to show restraint.
(Proverbs 23:4)

All hard work brings a profit, but mere talk leads only to poverty.
(Proverbs 14:23)

One who is slack in his work is brother to one who destroys.
(Proverbs 18:9)

He who works his land will have abundant food, but he
who chases fantasies lacks judgement.
(Proverbs 12:11)

*Do not work for food that spoils, but for food that endures to
eternal life, which the son of Man will give you.*
(John 6:27)

*As long as it is day, we must do the work of him who sent me.
Night is coming, when no one can work.*
(John 9:4)

PARENTING

See also:
Adolescent Guidance
Adolescent Rebellion
Child Abuse/Neglect
Children

Train a child in the way he should
go, and when he is old he will not
turn from it.
(Proverbs 22:6)

Fathers, do not embitter your children, or they will become discouraged.
(Colossians 3:21)

Fathers, do not exasperate your children; instead, bring
them up in the training and instruction of the Lord.
(Ephesians 6:4)

Pleasant words promote instruction.
(Proverbs 16:21)

A wise man's heart guides his mouth, and his lips promote instruction.
(Proverbs 16:23)

To show partiality in judging is not good.
(Proverbs 24:23)

He who fears the LORD has a secure fortress, and for his
children it will be a refuge.
(Proverbs 14:26)

Folly is bound up in the heart of a child, but the rod of
discipline will drive it far from him.
(Proverbs 22:15)

He who spares the rod hates his son, but he who loves
him is careful to discipline him.
(Proverbs 13:24)

The rod of correction imparts wisdom, but a child left to himself disgraces his mother.
(Proverbs 29:15)

Discipline your son, for in that there is hope; do not be a willing party to his death.
(Proverbs 19:18)

Discipline your son, and he will give you peace, he will bring delight to your soul.
(Proverbs 29:17)

Do not withhold discipline from a child; if you punish him with the rod, he will not die. Punish him with the rod and save his soul from death.
(Proverbs 23:13-14)

Sons are a heritage from the LORD, children a reward from him.
(Psalm 127:3)

The father of a righteous man has great joy; he who has a wise son delights in him.
(Proverbs 23:24)

Like arrows in the hands of a warrior are sons born in one's youth. Blessed is the man whose quiver is full of them.
(Psalm 127:4-5)

May the LORD make you increase, both you and your children. May you be blessed by the LORD, the Maker of heaven and earth.
(Psalm 115:14-15)

PEACE

See also:
Holy Spirit
Impatient
Love, By God
Protection
Refuge/Safety

The LORD blesses his people with peace.
(Psalm 29:11)

You know the message God sent to the
people of Israel, telling the good news
of peace through Jesus Christ, who is
Lord of all.
(Acts 10:36)

For unto us a child is born, to us a son is given, and the
government will be on his shoulders. And he will be
called Wonderful Counselor, Mighty God, Everlasting
Father, Prince of Peace.
(Isaiah 9:6)

He came and preached peace to you who were far away
and peace to those who were near.
(Ephesians 2:17)

I have told you these things so that in me you may have peace.
(John 16:33)

Peace I leave with you; my peace I give you.
(John 14:27)

Glory to God in the highest, and on earth peace to men
on whom his favor rests.
(Luke 2:14)

If only you had paid attention to my commands, your
peace would have been like a river, your righteousness
like the waves of the sea.
(Isaiah 48:18)

Great peace have they who love your law, and nothing can make them stumble.
(Psalm 119:165)

Let the peace of Christ rule in your hearts, since as members of one body you were called to peace.
(Colossians 3:15)

Turn from evil and do good; seek peace and pursue it.
(Psalm 34:14)

Let us therefore make every effort to do what leads to peace and to mutual edification.
(Romans 14:19)

Make every effort to keep the unity of the Spirit through the bond of peace.
(Ephesians 4:3)

Peacemakers who sow in peace raise a harvest of righteousness.
(James 3:18)

If it is possible, as far as it depends on you, live at peace with everyone.
(Romans 12:18)

Grace and peace to you from God our Father and the Lord Jesus Christ.
(Philippians 1:2)

Now may the Lord of peace Himself give you peace at all times and in every way.
(2 Thessalonians 3:16)

The God of peace be with you all. Amen.
(Romans 15:33)

PERSECUTION

See also:
Church
Witness

Do not be surprised, my brothers, if the
world hates you.
(1 John 3:13)

If the world hates you, keep in mind that it hated me first.
(John 15:18)

*No servant is greater than his master. If they persecuted me,
they will persecute you also.*
(John 15:20)

*All men will hate you because of me, but he who stands firm to
the end will be saved.*
(Mark 13:13)

Christ suffered for you, leaving you an example, that you
should follow in his steps.
(1 Peter 2:21)

Bless those who persecute you; bless and do not curse.
(Romans 12:14)

Rejoice that you participate in the sufferings of Christ, so
that you may be overjoyed when his glory is revealed.
(1 Peter 4:13)

Consider it pure joy, my brothers, whenever you face
trials of many kinds, because you know that the testing
of your faith develops perseverance.
(James 1:2-3)

We are hard pressed on every side, but not crushed;
perplexed, but not in despair; persecuted, but not abandoned; struck down, but not destroyed.
(2 Corinthians 4:8-9)

If you suffer for doing good and you endure it, this is
commendable before God.
(1 Peter 2:20)

It is better, if it is God's will, to suffer for doing good
than for doing evil.
(1 Peter 3:17)

If you suffer as a Christian, do not be ashamed, but
praise God that you bear that name.
(1 Peter 4:16)

If you are insulted because of the name of Christ, you are
blessed, for the Spirit of Glory and of God rests on you.
(1 Peter 4:14)

*Blessed are you when men hate you, when they exclude you
and insult you and reject your name as evil, because of the Son
of Man.*
(Luke 6:22)

Do not fear the reproach of men or be terrified by their
insults.
(Isaiah 51:7)

Though the arrogant have smeared me with lies, I keep
your precepts with all my heart.
(Psalm 119:69)

*Woe to you when all men speak well of you, for that is how
their fathers treated the false prophets.*
(Luke 6:26)

In fact, everyone who wants to live a godly life in Christ
Jesus will be persecuted, while evil men and impostors
will go from bad to worse, deceiving and being deceived.
(2 Timothy 3:12-13)

So then, those who suffer according to God's will should commit themselves to the faithful Creator and continue to do good.
(1 Peter 4:19)

For it has been granted to you on behalf of Christ not only to believe on him, but also to suffer for him.
(Philippians 1:29)

Dear friends, do not be surprised if the painful trial you are suffering, as though something strange were happening to you. But rejoice that you participate in the sufferings of Christ, so that you may be overjoyed when His glory is revealed.
(1 Peter 4:12-13)

Blessed are you when people insult you, persecute you and falsely say all kinds of evil against you because of me. Rejoice and be glad, because great is your reward in heaven.
(Matthew 5:11-12)

PLANS

See also:
Chosen/Elect
Occupation/Job/Work
Servant
Will of God

Commit to the LORD whatever
you do, and your plans will
succeed.
(Proverbs 16:3)

There is no wisdom, no insight, no plan than can succeed
against the LORD.
(Proverbs 21:30)

The LORD works out everything for His own ends.
(Proverbs 16:4)

Unless the LORD builds the house, its builders labor in
vain.
(Psalm 127:1)

Many are the plans in a man's heart, but it is the LORD's
purpose that prevails.
(Proverbs 19:21)

In his heart a man plans his course, but the LORD determines his steps.
(Proverbs 16:9)

Now listen, you who say, "Today or tomorrow we will
go to this or that city, spend a year there, carry on business and make money." Why, you do not even know
what will happen tomorrow.
(James 4:13-14)

What is your life? You are a mist that appears for a little
while and then vanishes. Instead, you ought to say, "If it
is the Lord's will, we will live and do this or that."
(James 4:15)

The plans of the LORD stand firm forever, the purposes of his heart through all generations.
(Psalm 33:11)

And we know that in all things God works for the good of those who love him, who have been called according to his purpose.
(Romans 8:28)

If God is for us, who can be against us?
(Romans 8:31)

He who began a good work in you will carry it on to completion until the day of Christ Jesus.
(Philippians 1:6)

When a man's ways are pleasing to the LORD, he makes even his enemies live at peace with him.
(Proverbs 16:7)

Commit your way to the LORD; trust in him and he will do this: He will make your righteousness shine like the dawn, the justice of your cause like the noonday sun.
(Psalm 37:5-6)

Woe to those who go to great depths to hide their plans from the LORD, who do their work in darkness and think, "Who sees us? Who will know?"
(Isaiah 29:15)

There is a way that seems right to a man, but in the end it leads to death.
(Proverbs 14:12)

All a man's ways seem innocent to him, but motives are weighed by the LORD.
(Proverbs 16:2)

God made mankind upright, but men have gone in search of many schemes.
(Ecclesiastes 7:29)

The highway of the upright avoids evil; he who guards his way guards his life.
(Proverbs 16:17)

He who works his land will have abundant food, but the one who chases fantasies will have his fill of poverty.
(Proverbs 28:19)

A faithful man will be richly blessed, but one eager to get rich, will not go unpunished.
(Proverbs 28:20)

Dishonest money dwindles away, but he who gathers money little by little makes it grow.
(Proverbs 13:11)

Be very careful, then, how you live — not as unwise but as wise, making the most of every opportunity, because the days are evil.
(Ephesians 5:15-16)

Every prudent man acts out of knowledge, but a fool exposes his folly.
(Proverbs 13:16)

The wisdom of the prudent is to give thought to their ways, but the folly of fools is deception.
(Proverbs 14:8)

A prudent man sees danger and takes refuge, but the simple keep going and suffer for it.
(Proverbs 22:3)

A simple man believes anything, but a prudent man
gives thought to his steps.
(Proverbs 14:15)

Plans fail for lack of counsel, but with many advisers
they succeed.
(Proverbs 15:22)

The plans of the diligent lead to profit as surely as haste
leads to poverty.
(Proverbs 21:5)

May he give you the desire of your heart and make all
your plans succeed.
(Psalm 20:4)

POVERTY

See also:
Envy/Jealousy
Greedy/Stingy
Money
Riches, Beware Of
Riches, True
Worldly

Better a poor man whose walk is blameless, than a rich man whose ways are perverse.
(Proverbs 28:6)

Better a little with the fear of the LORD than great wealth with turmoil.
(Proverbs 15:16)

Yet I am poor and needy; come quickly to me, O God. You are my help and my deliverer; O LORD, do not delay.
(Psalm 70:5)

You have been a refuge for the poor, a refuge for the needy in his distress, a shelter from the storm and a shade from the heat.
(Isaiah 25:4)

You rescue the poor from those too strong for them, the poor and needy from those who rob them.
(Psalm 35:10)

The needy will not always be forgotten, nor the hope of the afflicted ever perish.
(Psalm 9:18)

I know that the LORD secures justice for the poor and upholds the cause of the needy.
(Psalm 140:12)

He will take pity on the weak and the needy and save the needy from death.
(Psalm 72:13)

He raises the poor from the dust and lifts the needy from the ash heap; he seats them with princes, with the princes of their people.
(Psalm 113:7-8)

A rich man may be wise in his own eyes, but a poor man who has discernment sees through him.
(Proverbs 28:11)

The poor man and the oppressor have this in common: The LORD gives sight to the eyes of both.
(Proverbs 29:13)

He who mocks the poor shows contempt for their Maker.
(Proverbs 17:5)

The righteous care about justice for the poor, but the wicked have no such concern.
(Proverbs 29:7)

Speak up for those who cannot speak for themselves, for the rights of all who are destitute.
(Proverbs 31:8)

Defend the rights of the poor and needy.
(Proverbs 31:9)

Give me neither poverty nor riches, but give me only my daily bread. Otherwise, I may have too much and disown you and say, "Who is the LORD?" Or I may become poor and steal, and so dishonor the name of my God.
(Proverbs 30:8-9)

Therefore I tell you, do not worry about your life, what you will eat or drink; or about your body, what you will wear. Is not life more important than food, and the body more important than clothes?
(Matthew 6:25)

The LORD is my shepherd, I shall not be in want.
(Psalm 23:1)

You prepare a table before me in the presence of my enemies. You anoint my head with oil; my cup overflows.
(Psalm 23:5)

PRAISE HIM

See also:
Blessings
Joy
Sing Praises
Thankful
Worship

O LORD, our Lord, how majestic is
your name in all the earth!
(Psalm 8:1)

I will extol the LORD at all times; his praise will always be
on my lips.
(Psalm 34:1)

I will praise you, O LORD, with all my heart; I will tell of
all your wonders. I will be glad and rejoice in you; I will
sing praise to your name, O Most High.
(Psalm 9:1-2)

My tongue will speak of your righteousness and of your
praises all day long.
(Psalm 35:28)

I will praise you forever for what you have done.
(Psalm 52:9)

I will praise you, O Lord, among the nations; I will sing
of you among the peoples.
(Psalm 57:9)

Like your name, O God, your praise reaches to the ends
of the earth.
(Psalm 48:10)

From the rising of the sun to the place where it sets, the
name of the LORD is to be praised.
(Psalm 113:3)

Be exalted, O God, above the heavens; let your glory be
over all the earth.
(Psalm 57:11)

Let heaven and earth praise him, the seas and all that
move in them.
(Psalm 69:34)

Let the sea resound, and everything in it, the world and
all who live in it.
(Psalm 98:7)

Praise the LORD, all his heavenly hosts, you his servants
who do his will.
(Psalm 103:21)

Praise the LORD, O my soul; all my inmost being, praise
his holy name.
(Psalm 103:1)

I will praise you, O Lord my God, with all my heart; I
will glorify your name forever.
(Psalm 86:12)

For great is the LORD and most worthy of praise.
(Psalm 96:4)

Glorious and majestic are his deeds, and his righteousness endures forever.
(Psalm 111:3)

You are worthy, our Lord and God, to receive glory and
honor and power.
(Revelation 4:11)

To him belongs eternal praise.
(Psalm 111:10)

Let the name of the LORD be praised, both now and
forevermore.
(Psalm 113:2)

Let every creature praise his holy name for ever and ever.
(Psalm 145:21)

May his name endure forever; may it continue as long as
the sun.
(Psalm 72:17)

Let them praise his name with dancing and make music
to him with tambourine and harp.
(Psalm 149:3)

The heavens proclaim his righteousness, and all the
peoples see his glory.
(Psalm 97:6)

Praise the LORD, all his works everywhere in his dominion. Praise the LORD, O my soul.
(Psalm 103:22)

May my lips overflow with praise, for you teach me your
decrees.
(Psalm 119:171)

Praise be to his glorious name forever; may the whole
earth be filled with his glory. Amen and Amen.
(Psalm 72:19)

Praise the LORD from the heavens, praise him in the
heights above.
(Psalm 148:1)

My tongue will tell of your righteous acts all day long.
(Psalm 71:24)

The LORD reigns, he is robed in majesty.
(Psalm 93:1)

My mouth is filled with your praise, declaring your splendor all day long.
(Psalm 71:8)

I will praise your name, O Lord, for it is good.
(Psalm 54:6)

O Lord, open my lips, and my mouth will declare your praise.
(Psalm 51:15)

My mouth will tell of your righteousness, of your salvation all day long, though I know not its measure.
(Psalm 71:15)

Praise the Lord, you his angels, you mighty ones who do his bidding, who obey his word.
(Psalm 103:20)

In God we make our boast all day long, and we will praise your name forever.
(Psalm 44:8)

I will be exalted among the nations, I will be exalted in the earth.
(Psalm 46:10)

PRAYER, ANSWERS TO

See also:
Blessings
Prayer, Hindrance To
Prayer, How To
Thankful

The prayer of a righteous man is powerful and effective.
(James 5:16)

This is the confidence we have in approaching God: that if we ask anything according to his will, he hears us.
(1 John 5:14)

And if we know that he hears us — whatever we ask — we know that we have what we asked of him.
(1 John 5:15)

And I will do whatever you ask in my name, so that the Son may bring glory to the Father.
(John 14:13)

You may ask me for anything in my name, and I will do it.
(John 14:14)

I tell you the truth, my Father will give you whatever you ask in my name.
(John 16:23)

Ask and you will receive, and your joy will be complete.
(John 16:24)

For everyone who asks receives; he who seeks finds; and to hin who knocks,the door will be opened.
(Luke 11:10)

If you then, though you are evil, know how to give good gifts to your children, how much more will your Father in heaven give the Holy Spirit to those who ask him!
(Luke 11:13)

Your Father knows what you need before you ask him.
(Matthew 6:8)

Therefore I tell you, whatever you ask for in prayer, believe that you have received it, and it will be yours.
(Mark 11:24)

Again, I tell you that if two of you on earth agree about anything you ask for, it will be done for you by my Father in heaven. For where two or three come together in my name, there am I with them.
(Matthew 18:19-20)

If you believe, you will receive whatever you ask for in prayer.
(Matthew 21:22)

The eyes of the Lord are on the righteous and his ears are attentive to their cry.
(Psalm 34:15)

The Lord will hear when I call to him.
(Psalm 4:3)

I call on you, O God, for you will answer me; give ear to me and hear my prayer.
(Psalm 17:6)

The righteous cry out, and the Lord hears them; he delivers them from all their troubles.
(Psalm 34:17)

When I called, you answered me; you made me bold and stouthearted.
(Psalm 138:3)

But I pray to you, O Lord, in the time of your favor; in your great love, O God, answer me with your sure salvation.
(Psalm 69:13)

Hear, O LORD, and answer me, for I am poor and needy.
(Psalm 86:1)

Those who sow in tears will reap with songs of joy.
(Psalm 126:5)

I love the LORD, for he heard my voice; he heard my cry
for mercy. Because he turned his ear to me, I will call on
him as long as I live.
(Psalm 116:1-2)

May the LORD grant all your requests.
(Psalm 20:5)

PRAYER, HINDRANCE TO

See also:
Prayer, Answers To
Prayer, How To

If I had cherished sin in my heart, the LORD would not have listened.
(Psalm 66:18)

If anyone turns a deaf ear to the law, even his prayers are detestable.
(Proverbs 28:9)

If you remain in me and my words remain in you, ask whatever you wish, and it will be given to you.
(John 15:7)

But your iniquities have separated you from your God; your sins have hidden his face from you, so that he will not hear.
(Isaiah 59:2)

Dear friends, if our hearts do not condemn us, we have confidence before God and receive from him anything we ask, because we obey his commands and do what pleases him.
(1 John 3:21-22)

And without faith it is impossible to please God, because anyone who comes to him must believe that he exists and that he rewards those who earnestly seek him.
(Hebrews 11:6)

And when you stand praying, if you hold anything against anyone, forgive him, so that your Father in heaven may forgive you your sins.
(Mark 11:25)

The Lord says: "These people come near to me with their mouth and honor me with their lips, but their hearts are far from me. Their worship of me is made up only of rules taught by men."
(Isaiah 29:13)

When you ask, you do not receive, because you ask with wrong motives, that you may spend what you get on your pleasures.
(James 4:3)

PRAYER, HOW TO

See also:
Lord's Prayer
Meditation
Prayer, Answers To
Prayer, Hindrance To

I urge, then, first of all, that requests, prayers, intercession and thanksgiving be made for everyone — for kings and all those in authority, that we may live peaceful and quiet lives in all godliness and holiness.
(1 Timothy 2:1-2)

And pray in the Spirit on all occasions with all kinds of prayers and requests. With this in mind, be alert and always keep on praying for all the saints.
(Ephesians 6:18)

Devote yourselves to prayer, being watchful and thankful.
(Colossians 4:2)

Jesus went out to the mountainside to pray, and spent the night praying to God.
(Luke 6:12)

Very early in the morning, while it was still dark, Jesus got up, left the house, and went off to a solitary place, where he prayed.
(Mark 1:35)

About eight days after Jesus said this, he took Peter, John and James with him and went up onto a mountain to pray.
(Luke 9:28)

When you pray, say: "Father, hallowed be your name, your kingdom come. Give us each day our daily bread. Forgive us our sins, for we also forgive everyone who sins against us. And lead us not into temptation."
(Luke 11:2-4)

Then Jesus told His disciples a parable to show them that they should always pray and not give up.
(Luke 18:1)

And when you pray, do not be like the hypocrites, for they love to pray standing in the synagogues and on the street corners to be seen by men.
(Matthew 6:5)

But when you pray, go into your room, close the door and pray to your Father, who is unseen. Then your Father, who sees what is done in secret, will reward you.
(Matthew 6:6)

And when you pray, do not keep babbling like pagans, for they think they will be heard because of their many words.
(Matthew 6:7)

Do not be quick with your mouth, do not be hasty in your heart to utter anything before God. God is in heaven and you are on earth, so let your words be few.
(Ecclesiastes 5:2)

The LORD detests the sacrifice of the wicked, but the prayer of the upright pleases him.
(Proverbs 15:8)

In the morning, O LORD, you hear my voice; in the morning I lay my requests before you and wait in expectation.
(Psalm 5:3)

O LORD, the God who saves me, day and night I cry out before you. May my prayer come before you; turn your ear to my cry.
(Psalm 88:1)

Listen to my cry for help, my King and my God, for to you I pray.
(Psalm 5:2)

The Spirit helps us in our weakness. We do not know what we ought to pray for, but the Spirit himself intercedes for us with groans that words cannot express.
(Romans 8:26)

PREJUDICE

See also:
Boastful
Conceit
Humility
Pride
Riches, Beware Of
Servant

My brothers, as believers in our glorious Lord Jesus Christ, don't show favoritism.
(James 2:1)

God does not show favoritism but accepts men from every nation who fear him and do what is right.
(Acts 10:34-35)

Do not mistreat an alien or oppress him.
(Exodus 22:21)

You are all sons of God through faith in Christ Jesus, for all of you who were baptized into Christ have clothed yourselves with Christ. There is neither Jew nor Greek, slave nor free, male nor female, for you are all one in Christ Jesus.
(Galatians 3:26-29)

For there is no difference between Jew and Gentile—the same Lord is Lord of all and richly blesses all who call on him, for, "Everyone who calls on the name of the Lord will be saved."
(Romans 10:12-13)

But if you show favoritism, you sin and are convicted by the law as lawbreakers.
(James 2:9)

And masters, treat your slaves in the same way. Do not threaten them, since you know that he who is both their Master and yours is in heaven, and there is no favoritism with him.
(Ephesians 6:9)

God does not show favoritism.
(Romans 2:11)

God does not judge by external appearance.
(Galatians 2:6)

Stop judging by mere appearances, and make a right judgment.
(John 7:24)

Accept one another, then, just as Christ accepted you, in order to bring praise to God.
(Romans 15:7)

PRIDE

The LORD detests all the proud
of heart.
(Proverbs 16:5)

He mocks proud mockers but
gives grace to the humble.
(Proverbs 3:34)

He has scattered those who are proud in their inmost
thoughts. He has brought down rulers from their
thrones, but has lifted up the humble.
(Luke 1:51-52)

The LORD Almighty has a day in store for all the proud
and lofty, for all that is exalted (and they will be humbled).
(Isaiah 2:12)

Pride goes before destruction, a haughty spirit before a
fall.
(Proverbs 16:18)

The arrogance of man will be brought low and the pride
of men humbled.
(Isaiah 2:17)

Before his downfall a man's heart is proud, but humility
comes before honor.
(Proverbs 18:12)

God opposes the proud but gives grace to the humble.
(James 4:6)

Pride only breeds quarrels, but wisdom is found in those who take advice.
(Proverbs 13:10)

When pride comes, then comes disgrace, but with humility comes wisdom.
(Proverbs 11:2)

Whoever has haughty eyes and a proud heart, him will I not endure.
(Psalm 101:5)

Though the LORD is on high, he looks upon the lowly, but the proud he knows from afar.
(Psalm 138:6)

PROMISCUITY

See also:
Homosexuality
Lust
Prostitution
Sex, Normal
Sex, Perverted

The body is not meant for sexual
immorality, but for the Lord, and
the Lord for the body.
(1 Corinthians 6:13)

Flee from sexual immorality. All other sins a man commits are outside his body, but he who sins sexually sins
against his own body.
(1 Corinthians 6:18)

Do you not know that your body is a temple of the Holy
Spirit, who is in you, whom you have received from
God? You are not your own; you were bought at a price.
Therefore honor God with your body.
(1 Corinthians 6:19-20)

We should not commit sexual immorality.
(1 Corinthians 10:8)

For God did not call us to be impure, but to live a holy life.
(1 Thessalonians 4:7)

You are to abstain from...sexual immorality.
(Acts 15:29)

Put to death, therefore, whatever belongs to your earthly
nature: sexual immorality, impurity, lust, evil desires and
greed, which is idolatry.
(Colossians 3:5)

But the cowardly, the unbelieving, the vile, the murderers, the sexually immoral, those who practice magic arts,
the idolaters and all liars — their place will be in the fiery
lake of burning sulfur. This is the second death.
(Revelation 21:8)

For of this you can be sure: No immoral, impure or greedy person — such a man is an idolater — has any inheritance in the kingdom of Christ and of God.
(Ephesians 5:5)

But among you there must not be even a hint of sexual immorality, or of any kind of impurity, or of greed, because these are improper for God's holy people.
(Ephesians 5:3)

The acts of the sinful nature are obvious: sexual immorality, impurity and debauchery; idolatry and witchcraft; hatred, discord, jealousy, fits of rage, selfish ambition, dissensions, factions and envy; drunkenness, orgies, and the like.
(Galatians 5:19-21)

I warn you, as I did before, that those who live like this will not inherit the kingdom of God.
(Galatians 5:21)

PROSTITUTION

See also:
Homosexuality
Lust
Promiscuity
Sex, Normal
Sex, Perverted

Do you not know that your bodies are members of Christ himself? Shall I then take the members of Christ and unite them with a prostitute? Never!
(1 Corinthians 6:15)

Do you not know that he who unites himself with a prostitute is one with her in body? For it is said, "The two will become one flesh." But he who unites himself with the Lord is one with the spirit.
(1 Corinthians 6:16-17)

Do not degrade your daughter by making her a prostitute, or the land will turn to prostitution and be filled with wickedness.
(Leviticus 19:29)

Do not lust in your heart after her beauty or let her captivate you with her eyes, for the prostitute reduces you to a loaf of bread, and the adulteress preys upon your very life.
(Proverbs 6:25-26)

Do not let your heart turn to her ways or stray into her paths. Many are the victims she has brought down; her slain are a mighty throng.
(Proverbs 7:25-26)

Her house is a highway to the grave, leading down to the chambers of death.
(Proverbs 7:27)

With persuasive words she led him astray; she seduced him with her smooth talk.
(Proverbs 7:21)

All at once he followed her like an ox going to the slaughter, like a deer stepping into a noose till an arrow pierces his liver, like a bird darting into a snare, little knowing it will cost him his life.
(Proverbs 7:22-23)

For a prostitute is a deep pit and a wayward wife is a narrow well.
(Proverbs 23:27)

A man who loves wisdom brings joy to his father, but a companion of prostitutes squanders his wealth.
(Proverbs 29:3)

Has no one condemned you? "No one, sir," she said. *Then neither do I condemn you,* Jesus declared, *Go now and leave your life of sin.*
(John 8:10-11)

PROTECTION

See also:
God, All Powerful
Help
Mercy
Refuge/Safety
Strength
Trust
Weakness

The LORD is my rock, my fortress and my deliverer; my God is my rock, in whom I take refuge. He is my shield and the horn of my salvation, my stronghold.
(Psalm 18:2)

Deliver me from my enemies, O God; protect me from those who rise up against me.
(Psalm 59:1)

"Because of the oppression of the weak and the groaning of the needy, I will now arise," says the LORD. "I will protect them from those who malign them."
(Psalm 12:5)

O LORD, you will keep us safe and protect us from such people forever.
(Psalm 12:7)

You are a shield around me, O LORD; you bestow glory on me and lift up my head.
(Psalm 3:3)

The LORD is my strength and my shield; my heart trusts in him, and I am helped.
(Psalm 28:7)

He is a shield for all who take refuge in him.
(Psalm 18:30)

Therefore put on the full armor of God, so that when the day of evil comes, you may be able to stand your ground, and after you have done everything, to stand.
(Ephesians 6:13)

Stand firm then, with the belt of truth buckled around your waist, with the breastplate of righteousness in place, and with your feet fitted with the readiness that comes from the gospel of peace.
(Ephesians 6:14-15)

In addition to all this, take up the shield of faith, with which you can extinguish all the flaming arrows of the evil one. Take the helmet of salvation and the sword of the Spirit, which is the word of God.
(Ephesians 6:16-17)

PSALM 23

See also:
Anxiety/Worry
Death/Dying
Fear
Grief
Sickness
Sorrow
Suffering

The LORD is my shepherd, I shall not
be in want.
He makes me lie down in green pastures,
he leads me beside quiet waters,
he restores my soul.
He guides me in paths of righteousness
for his name's sake.
Even though I walk
through the valley of the shadow of death,
I will fear no evil,
for you are with me;
your rod and your staff,
they comfort me.
You prepare a table before me
in the presence of my enemies.
You anoint my head with oil;
my cup overflows.
Surely goodness and love will follow me
all the days of my life,
and I will dwell in the house of the LORD forever.

REBUKE/ CORRECTION

See also:
Church
Discipline

Brothers, if someone is caught in a sin, you who are spiritual should restore him gently. But watch yourself, or you also may be tempted.
(Galatians 6:1)

Rebuke your neighbor frankly so you will not share in his guilt.
(Leviticus 19:17)

He who rebukes a man will in the end gain more favor than he who has a flattering tongue.
(Proverbs 28:23)

Those whom I love I rebuke and discipline. So be earnest and repent.
(Revelation 3:19)

Stern discipline awaits him who leaves the path; he who hates correction will die.
(Proverbs 15:10)

Rebuke a wise man and he will love you. Instruct a wise man and he will be wiser still; teach a righteous man and he will add to his learning.
(Proverbs 9:8-9)

A rebuke impresses a man of discernment more than a hundred lashes a fool.
(Proverbs 17:10)

Rebuke a discerning man, and he will gain knowledge.
(Proverbs 19:25)

He who listens to life-giving rebuke will be at home among the wise.
(Proverbs 15:31)

Whoever gives heed to instruction prospers, and blessed is he who trusts in the LORD.
(Proverbs 16:20)

It is better to heed a wise man's rebuke than to listen to the song of fools.
(Ecclesiastes 7:5)

A man who remains stiff-necked after many rebukes will suddenly be destroyed — without remedy.
(Proverbs 29:1)

Preach the Word; be prepared in season and out of season; correct, rebuke and encourage — with great patience and careful instruction.
(2 Timothy 4:2)

REFUGE/SAFETY

See also:
God, All Loving
Help
Mercy
Protection
Strength
Weakness

Blessed are all who take refuge
in Him.
(Psalm 2:12)

The eternal God is your refuge, and
underneath are the everlasting arms.
(Deuteronomy 33:27)

You are my hiding place; you will protect me from
trouble and surround me with songs of deliverance.
(Psalm 32:7)

Spread your protection over them, that those who love
your name may rejoice in you.
(Psalm 5:11)

He will cover you with his feathers, and under his wings
you will find refuge.
(Psalm 91:4)

It is good to be near God.
(Psalm 73:28)

Hide me in the shadow of your wings from the wicked
who assail me, from my mortal enemies who surround
me.
(Psalm 17:8-9)

Both high and low among men find refuge in the shadow
of your wings.
(Psalm 36:7)

He is a shield for all who take refuge in him.
(2 Samuel 22:31)

In the shelter of your presence you hide them from the intrigues of men; in your dwelling you keep them safe from accusing tongues.
(Psalm 31:20)

Keep me safe, O God, for in you I take refuge.
(Psalm 16:1)

Rescue me from my enemies, O LORD, for I hide myself in you.
(Psalm 143:9)

Save and deliver me from all who pursue me.
(Psalm 7:1)

Turn your ear to me, come quickly to my rescue.
(Psalm 31:2)

The LORD is my rock, my fortress and my deliverer.
(2 Samuel 22:2)

For you have been my refuge, a strong tower against the foe.
(Psalm 61:3)

My God is my rock, in whom I take refuge, my shield and the horn of my salvation.
(2 Samuel 22:3)

The man who makes me his refuge will inherit the land and possess my holy mountain.
(Isaiah 57:13)

It is better to take refuge in the LORD than to trust in man.
(Psalm 118:8)

I long to dwell in your tent forever.
(Psalm 61:4)

My eyes are fixed on you, O Sovereign LORD.
(Psalm 141:8)

Taste and see that the LORD is good; blessed is the man
who takes refuge in him.
(Psalm 34:8)

The LORD will rescue me from every evil attack and will
bring me safely to his heavenly kingdom. To him be
glory for ever and ever. Amen.
(2 Timothy 4:18)

REPENT

See also:
Belief
Born Again
Confession
End Times
Eternal Life
Salvation
Second Coming

*The kingdom of God is near. Repent and
believe the good news!*
(Mark 1:15)

Turn to me and be saved, all you ends
of the earth; for I am God, and there is
no other.
(Isaiah 45:22)

Let him turn to the LORD, and he will have mercy on him,
and to our God, for he will freely pardon.
(Isaiah 55:7)

Repent and be baptized, every one of you, in the name of
Jesus Christ for the forgiveness of your sins. And you
will receive the gift of the Holy Spirit.
(Acts 2:38)

Those who oppose him he must gently instruct, in the
hope that God will grant them repentance leading them
to a knowledge of the truth, and that they will come to
their senses and escape from the trap of the devil, who
has taken them captive to do his will.
(2 Timothy 2:25-26)

Repent, then, and turn to God, so that your sins may be
wiped out, that times of refreshing may come from the
Lord, and that he may send the Christ, who has been
appointed for you — even Jesus.
(Acts 3:19-20)

I have not come to call the righteous, but sinners to repentance.
(Luke 5:32)

There will be more rejoicing in heaven over one sinner who repents than over ninety-nine righteous persons who do not need to repent.
(Luke 15:7)

They went out and preached that people should repent.
(Mark 6:12)

Come back to your senses as you ought, and stop sinning.
(1 Corinthians 15:34)

RICHES, BEWARE OF

See also:
Envy/Jealousy
Giving
Greedy/Stingy
Money
Poverty
Riches, True
Self-Sacrifice
Worldly

Though your riches increase, do
not set your heart on them.
(Psalm 62:10)

A man who has riches without understanding is like the
beasts that perish.
(Psalm 49:20)

Cast but a glance at riches, and they are gone, for they will
surely sprout wings and fly off to the sky like an eagle.
(Proverbs 23:5)

Be sure you know the condition of your flocks, give
careful attention to your herds; for riches do not endure
forever, and a crown is not secure for all generations.
(Proverbs 27:23-24)

Do not be overawed when a man grows rich, when the splendor of
his house increases; for he will take nothing with him when he dies.
(Psalm 49:16-17)

For a man may do his work with wisdom, knowledge
and skill, and then he must leave all he owns to someone
who has not worked for it.
(Ecclesiastes 2:21)

Naked I came from my mother's womb, and naked I will depart.
(Job 1:20)

*The time came when the beggar died and the angels carried him
to Abraham's side. The rich man also died and was buried.*
(Luke 16:22)

For all can see that wise men die; the foolish and sense-less alike perish and leave their wealth to others.
(Psalm 49:10)

But God said to him, "You fool! This very night your life will be demanded from you. Then who will get what you have prepared for yourself?" This is how it will be for anyone who stores up things for himself but is not rich toward God.
(Luke 12:20-21)

Woe to you who are well fed now, for you will go hungry.
(Luke 6:25)

Woe to you who laugh now, for you will mourn and weep.
(Luke 6:25)

Command those who are rich in this present world not to be arrogant nor to put their hope in wealth, which is so uncertain, but put their hope in God, who richly provides us with everything for our enjoyment.
(1 Timothy 6:17)

Command them to do good, to be rich in good deeds, and to be generous and willing to share. In this way they will lay up treasure for themselves as a firm foundation for the coming age, so that they may take hold of the life that is truly life.
(1 Timothy 6:18-19)

RICHES, TRUE

See also:
Blessings
Envy/Jealousy
Giving
Greedy/Stingy
Money
Poverty
Riches, Beware Of
Worldly

Sell your possessions and give to the poor. Provide purses for yourselves that will not wear out, a treasure in heaven that will not be exhausted, where no thief comes near and no moth destroys.
(Luke 12:33)

For where your treasure is, there your heart will be also.
(Luke 12:34)

Whatever was to my profit I now consider loss for the sake of Christ.
(Philippians 3:7)

I consider everything a loss compared to the surpassing greatness of knowing Christ Jesus my Lord, for whose sake I have lost all things. I consider them rubbish, that I may gain Christ and be found in him.
(Philippians 3:8-9)

I have learned the secret of being content in any and every situation, whether well fed or hungry, whether living in plenty or in want.
(Philippians 4:12)

Wealth is worthless in the day of wrath, but righteousness delivers from death.
(Proverbs 11:4)

Whoever trusts in his riches will fall, but the righteous will thrive like a green leaf.
(Proverbs 11:28)

But you, man of God, flee from all this, and pursue righteousness, godliness, faith, love, endurance and gentleness.
(1 Timothy 6:11)

Better the little that the righteous have than the wealth of many wicked; for the power of the wicked will be broken, but the LORD upholds the righteous.
(Psalm 37:16-17)

Has not God chosen those who are poor in the eyes of the world to be rich in faith and to inherit the kingdom he promised those who love him?
(James 2:5)

For you know the grace of our Lord Jesus Christ, that though he was rich, yet for your sakes he became poor, so that you through his poverty might become rich.
(2 Corinthians 8:9)

You will be made rich in every way so that you can be generous on every occasion, and through us your generosity will result in thanksgiving to God.
(2 Corinthians 9:11)

How much better to get wisdom than gold, to choose understanding rather than silver!
(Proverbs 16:16)

And do not set your heart on what you will eat or drink; do not worry about it. For the pagan world runs after all such things, and your Father knows that you need them.
(Luke 12:29-30)

But seek first his kingdom and his righteousness, and all these things will be given to you as well.
(Matthew 6:33)

RIGHTEOUS

> **See also:**
> Action
> Blessings
> Disobedience
> Gifts, Physical/Material
> Obedience

Then the righteous will shine like the sun in the kingdom of their Father. He who has ears, let him hear.
(Matthew 13:43)

Listen to me, you stubborn-hearted, you who are far from righteousness. I am bringing my righteousness near, it is not far away.
(Isaiah 46:12-13)

This is what the LORD says: Do what is just and right.
(Jeremiah 22:3)

Whatever happens, conduct yourselves in a manner worthy of the gospel of Christ.
(Philippians 1:27)

If you know that he is righteous, you know that everyone who does what is right has been born of him.
(1 John 2:29)

When the storm has swept by, the wicked are gone, but the righteous stand firm forever.
(Proverbs 10:25)

The righteousness of the blameless makes a straight way for them, but the wicked are brought down by their own wickedness.
(Proverbs 11:5)

The light of the righteous shines brightly, but the lamp of the wicked is snuffed out.
(Proverbs 13:9)

Misfortune pursues the sinner, but prosperity is the
reward of the righteous.
(Proverbs 13:21)

The righteous eat to their hearts' content, but the stomach
of the wicked goes hungry.
(Proverbs 13:25)

The righteous will flourish like a palm tree, they will
grow like a cedar of Lebanon; planted in the house of the
LORD, they will flourish in the courts of our God.
(Psalm 92:12-13)

SALVATION

See also:
Belief
Born Again
Christ, Mission Of
Confession
Eternal Life
Faith
Grace
Repent

If you confess with your mouth,
"Jesus is Lord," and believe in
your heart that God raised him
from the dead, you will be saved.
(Romans 10:9)

At just the right time, when we were still powerless,
Christ died for the ungodly.
(Romans 5:6)

For the Son of Man came to seek and to save what was lost.
(Luke 19:10)

Since we have now been justified by his blood, how
much more shall we be saved from God's wrath through
him!
(Romans 5:9)

You were bought at a price; do not become slaves of men.
(1 Corinthians 7:23)

Now that you have been set free from sin and have
become slaves to God, the benefit you reap leads to
holiness, and the result is eternal life.
(Romans 6:22)

But if anybody does sin, we have one who speaks to the
Father in our defense — Jesus Christ, the Righteous One.
He is the atoning sacrifice for our sins, and not only for
ours but also for the sins of the whole world.
(1 John 2:1-2)

For you know that it was not with perishable things such
as silver or gold that you were redeemed from the empty

way of life handed down to you from your forefathers,
but with the precious blood of Christ, a lamb without
blemish or defect.
(1 Peter 1:18-19)

But now in Christ Jesus you who once were far away
have been brought near through the blood of Christ.
(Ephesians 2:13)

God our Savior...wants all men to be saved and to come
to a knowledge of the truth.
(1 Timothy 2:3-4)

Everyone who calls on the name of the Lord will be
saved.
(Acts 2:21)

I tell you, now is the time of God's favor, now is the day
of salvation.
(2 Corinthians 6:2)

O Lᴏʀᴅ, you brought me up from the grave; you spared
me from going down into the pit.
(Psalm 30:3)

I will give you thanks, for you answered me; you have
become my salvation.
(Psalm 118:21)

My soul faints with longing for your salvation.
(Psalm 119:81)

Save me, for I am yours.
(Psalm 119:94)

*To him who overcomes, I will give the right to sit with me on my throne,
just as I overcame and sat down with my Father on his throne.*
(Revelation 3:21)

SCRIPTURE/ WORD

See also:
Commandments
Meditation
Seeking
Ten Commandments
Truth

As for God, his way is perfect.
(2 Samuel 22:31)

Every word of God is flawless.
(Proverbs 30:5)

Like silver refined in a furnace of clay, purified seven times.
(Psalm 12:6)

The law of the LORD is perfect, reviving the soul.
(Psalm 19:7)

Do not add to his words, or he will rebuke you and prove you a liar.
(Proverbs 30:6)

It is easier for heaven and earth to disappear than for the least stroke of a pen to drop out of the Law.
(Luke 16:17)

The grass withers and the flowers fall, but the word of our God stands forever.
(Isaiah 40:8)

How sweet are your words to my taste, sweeter than honey to my mouth!
(Psalm 119:103)

When your words came, I ate them; they were my joy and my heart's delight, for I bear your name, O LORD God Almighty.
(Jeremiah 15:16)

The voice of the LORD is powerful; the voice of the LORD is majestic.
(Psalm 29:4)

I delight in your decrees.
(Psalm 119:16)

I will not neglect your word.
(Psalm 119:16)

I have hidden your word in my heart that I might not sin against you.
(Psalm 119:11)

Let me understand the teaching of your precepts; then I will meditate on your wonders.
(Psalm 119:27)

Preserve my life according to your word.
(Psalm 119:37)

I have put my hope in your laws.
(Psalm 119:43)

The law from your mouth is more precious to me than thousands of pieces of silver and gold.
(Psalm 119:72)

Your commands make me wiser than my enemies, for they are ever with me.
(Psalm 119:98)

I have chosen the way of truth; I have set my heart on your laws.
(Psalm 119:30)

Teach me, O LORD, to follow your decrees; then I will keep them to the end.
(Psalm 119:33)

The statutes you have laid down are righteous; they are
fully trustworthy.
(Psalm 119:138)

Your statutes are forever right; give me understanding
that I may live.
(Psalm 119:144)

All your words are true; all your righteous laws are
eternal.
(Psalm 119:160)

I wait for the LORD, my soul waits, and in his word I put
my hope.
(Psalm 130:5)

Your word, O LORD, is eternal; it stands firm in the heavens.
(Psalm 119:89)

SECOND COMING

See also:
End Times
Heaven
Repent

Just as man is destined to die once, and
after that face judgment, so Christ was
sacrificed once to take away the sins of
many people; and he will appear a second
time, not to bear sin, but to bring salvation
to those who are waiting for him.
(Hebrews 9:27-28)

*For the Son of Man in his day will be like the lightning, which
flashes and lights up the sky from one end to the other. But first
he must suffer many things and be rejected by this generation.*
(Luke 17:24-25)

Why do you stand here looking into the sky? This same
Jesus, who has been taken from you into heaven, will come
back in the same way you have seen him go into heaven.
(Acts 1:11)

For the Lord himself will come down from heaven, with a
loud command, with the voice of the archangel and with the
trumpet call of God, and the dead in Christ will rise first.
(1 Thessalonians 4:16)

*Do not be amazed at this, for a time is coming when all who are
in their graves will hear his voice and come out — those who
have done good will rise to live, and those who have done evil
will rise to be condemned.*
(John 5:28-29)

*At that time men will see the Son of Man coming in clouds
with great power and glory. And he will send his angels and
gather his elect from the four winds, from the ends of the earth
to the ends of the heavens.*
(Mark 13:26-27)

Our citizenship is in heaven. And we eagerly await a Savior from there, the Lord Jesus Christ, who, by the power that enables him to bring everything under his control, will transform our lowly bodies so that they will be like his glorious body.
(Philippians 3:20-21)

When he appears, we shall be like him, for we shall see him as he is. Everyone who has this hope in him purifies himself, just as he is pure.
(1 John 3:2-3)

He will wipe every tear from their eyes. There will be no more death or mourning or crying or pain, for the old order of things has passed away.
(Revelation 21:4)

The kingdom of heaven is near.
(Matthew 10:7)

Behold, I am coming soon!
(Revelation 22:7)

SEEKING

> **See also:**
> Confusion
> Light
> Scripture/Word
> Strength
> Trust

Look to the LORD and his strength;
seek his face always.
(Psalm 105:4)

Seek the LORD while he may be found; call on him while he is near.
(Isaiah 55:6)

As the deer pants for streams of water, so my soul pants for you, O God.
(Psalm 42:1)

This is what the LORD says: "Stand at the crossroads and look; ask for the ancient paths, ask where the good way is, and walk in it, and you will find rest for your souls."
(Jeremiah 6:16)

Ask and it will be given to you; seek and you will find; knock and the door will be opened to you.
(Luke 11:9)

For everyone who asks receives; he who seeks finds; and to him who knocks, the door will be opened.
(Luke 11:10)

God looks down from heaven on the sons of men to see if there are any who understand, any who seek God.
(Psalm 53:2)

I seek you with all my heart; do not let me stray from your commands.
(Psalm 119:10)

May all who seek you rejoice and be glad in you.
(Psalm 40:16)

Let the hearts of those who seek the LORD rejoice.
(Psalm 105:3)

SELF-ESTEEM, LOW

See also:
God, All Loving
God, Creator
Love, By God

Then God said, "Let us make man in our image, in our likeness, and let them rule over the fish of the sea and the birds of the air, over the livestock, over all the earth, and over all the creatures that move along the ground."
(Genesis 1:26)

So God created man in his own image, in the image of God he created him; male and female he created them.
(Genesis 1:27)

O LORD, you are our Father.
(Isaiah 64:8)

We are his offspring.
(Acts 17:28)

The Spirit of God has made me; the breath of the Almighty gives me life.
(Job 33:4)

Rich and poor have this in common: the LORD is the maker of them all.
(Proverbs 22:2)

And just as we have born the likeness of the earthly man, so shall we bear the likeness of the man from heaven.
(1 Corinthians 15:49)

And we, who with unveiled faces all reflect the Lord's glory, are being transformed into his likeness with ever-increasing glory, which comes from the Lord, who is the Spirit.
(2 Corinthians 3:18)

In this way, love is made complete among us so that we will have confidence on the day of judgment, because in this world we are like him.
(1 John 4:17)

For we are God's workmanship, created in Christ Jesus to do good works, which God prepared in advance for us to do.
(Ephesians 2:10)

And we are in him who is true — even in his Son Jesus Christ.
(1 John 5:20)

You made him ruler over the works of your hands; you put everything under his feet.
(Psalm 8:6)

The very hairs of your head are numbered.
(Luke 12:7)

When I consider your heavens, the work of your fingers, the moon and the stars, which you have set in place, what is man that you are mindful of him, and the son of man that you care for him?
(Psalm 8:3-4)

You made him a little lower than the heavenly beings and crowned him with glory and honor.
(Psalm 8:5)

SELF-SACRIFICE

See also:
Occupation/Job/Work
Plans
Servant
Will of God

If anyone would come after me, he must deny himself and take up his cross and follow me.
(Matthew 16:24)

He died for all, that those who live should no longer live for themselves but for him who died for them and was raised again.
(2 Corinthians 5:15)

You were taught, with regard to your former way of life, to put off your old self, which is being corrupted by its deceitful desires; to be made new in the attitude of your minds; and to put on the new self, created to be like God in true righteousness and holiness.
(Ephesians 4:22-24)

But for those who are self-seeking and who reject the truth and follow evil, there will be wrath and anger.
(Romans 2:8)

Any of you who does not give up everything he has cannot be my disciple.
(Luke 14:33)

If anyone comes to me and does not hate his father and mother, his wife and children, his brothers and sisters — yes, even his own life — he cannot be my disciple.
(Luke 14:26)

For whoever wants to save his life will lose it, but whoever loses his life for me and for the gospel will save it.
(Mark 8:35)

Whoever finds his life will lose it, and whoever loses his life for my sake will find it.
(Matthew 10:39)

For I am not seeking my own good but the good of many, so that they may be saved.
(1 Corinthians 10:33)

SERVANT

See also:
Humility
Occupation/Job/Work
Self-Sacrifice
Will Of God

Whoever wants to become great among you must be your servant, and whoever wants to be first must be slave of all.
(Mark 10:43-44)

For even the Son of Man did not come to be served, but to serve, and to give his life as a ransom for many.
(Mark 10:45)

Whoever serves me must follow me; and where I am, my servant also will be. My father will honor the one who serves me.
(John 12:26)

Fear the LORD and serve him faithfully with all your heart; consider what great things he has done for you.
(1 Samuel 12:24)

Live as free men, but do not use your freedom as a cover-up for evil; live as servants of God.
(1 Peter 2:16)

You, my brothers, were called to be free. But do not use your freedom to indulge the sinful nature; rather, serve one another in love.
(Galatians 5:13)

For he who was a slave when he was called by the Lord is the Lord's freedman; similarly, he who was a free man when he was called is Christ's slave.
(1 Corinthians 7:22)

Though I am free and belong to no man, I make myself a slave to everyone, to win as many as possible.
(1 Corinthians 9:19)

If anyone serves, he should do it with the strength God provides, so that in all things God may be praised through Jesus Christ.
(1 Peter 4:11)

I do not run like a man running aimlessly; I do not fight like a man beating the air. No, I beat my body and make it my slave so that after I have preached to others, I myself will not be disqualified for the prize.
(1 Corinthians 9:26-27)

If I were still trying to please men, I would not be a servant of Christ.
(Galatians 1:10)

What does the LORD your God ask of you but to fear the LORD your God, to walk in all his ways, to love him, to serve the LORD your God with all your heart and with all your soul, and to observe the LORD's commands and decrees.
(Deuteronomy 10:12-13)

I am your servant; give me discernment that I may understand your statutes.
(Psalm 119:125)

But if serving the LORD seems undesirable to you, then choose for yourselves this day whom you will serve....But as for me and my household, we will serve the LORD.
(Joshua 24:15)

I tell you the truth, no servant is greater than his master, nor is a messenger greater than the one who sent him.
(John 13:16)

If anyone wants to be first, he must be the very last, and the servant of all.
(Mark 9:35)

Whoever wants to become great among you must be your servant, and whoever wants to be first must be your slave.
(Matthew 20:26-27)

SEX, NORMAL

See also:
Adultery
Husbands
Marriage
Sex, Perverted
Wives

God blessed them and said to them,
"Be fruitful and increase in number;
fill the earth and subdue it."
(Genesis 1:28)

For this reason a man will leave his father and mother
and be united to his wife, and they will become one flesh.
(Genesis 2:24)

So they are no longer two, but one.
(Mark 10:8)

The husband should fulfill his marital duty to his wife,
and likewise the wife to her husband.
(1 Corinthians 7:3)

The wife's body does not belong to her alone but also to
her husband. In the same way, the husband's body does
not belong to him alone but also to his wife.
(1 Corinthians 7:4)

Do not deprive each other except by mutual consent and
for a time, so that you may devote yourselves to prayer.
Then come together again so that Satan will not tempt
you because of your lack of self-control.
(1 Corinthians 7:5)

Marriage should be honored by all, and the marriage bed
kept pure, for God will judge the adulterer and all the
sexually immoral.
(Hebrews 13:4)

Drink water from your own cistern, running water from
your own well.
(Proverbs 5:15)

May your fountain be blessed, and may you rejoice in the wife of your youth. A loving doe, a graceful deer — may her breasts satisfy you always, may you ever be captivated by her love.
(Proverbs 5:18-19)

SEX, PERVERTED

See also:
Homosexuality
Lust
Promiscuity
Prostitution
Sex, Normal

They have perverted their ways and
have forgotten the LORD their God.
(Jeremiah 3:21)

Having lost all sensitivity, they have given themselves
over to sensuality so as to indulge in every kind of impurity, with a continual lust for more.
(Ephesians 4:19)

I am afraid that when I come again my God will humble
me before you, and I will be grieved over many who
have sinned earlier and have not repented of the impurity, sexual sin and debauchery in which they have in-
dulged.
(2 Corinthians 12:21)

A woman must not wear men's clothing, nor a man wear
women's clothing, for the LORD your God detests anyone
who does this.
(Deuteronomy 22:5)

Cursed is the man who has sexual relations with any
animal. Then all the people shall say, "Amen!"
(Deuteronomy 27:21)

A woman must not present herself to an animal to have
sexual relations with it; that is a perversion.
(Leviticus 18:23)

Anyone who has sexual relations with an animal must be
put to death.
(Exodus 22:19)

Have nothing to do with the fruitless deeds of darkness,
but rather expose them. For it is shameful even to men-
tion what the disobedient do in secret.
(Ephesians 5:11-12)

Therefore, get rid of all moral filth and the evil that is so
prevalent and humbly accept the word planted in you,
which can save you.
(James 1:21)

Sodom and Gomorrah and the surrounding towns gave
themselves up to sexual immorality and perversion. They
serve as an example of those who suffer the punishment
of eternal fire.
(Jude 1:7)

Therefore God gave them over in the sinful desires of
their hearts to sexual impurity for the degrading of their
bodies with one another.
(Romans 1:24)

Since they did not think it worthwhile to retain the
knowledge of God, he gave them over to a depraved
mind, to do what ought not to be done.
(Romans 1:28)

Do not offer the parts of your body to sin, as instruments
of wickedness, but rather offer yourselves to God, as
those who have been brought from death to life; and
offer the parts of your body to him as instruments of
righteousness.
(Romans 6:13)

Don't you know that when you offer yourselves to someone
to obey him as slaves, you are slaves to the one whom you
obey — whether you are slaves to sin, which leads to death,
or to obedience, which leads to righteousness?
(Romans 6:16)

Just as you used to offer the parts of your body in slavery to impurity and to ever-increasing wickedness, so now offer them in slavery to righteousness leading to holiness.
(Romans 6:19)

Let us behave decently, as in the daytime, not in orgies and drunkenness, not in sexual immorality and debauchery, not in dissension and jealousy.
(Romans 13:13)

SICKNESS

See also:
Death/Dying
Grief
Hardship
Help
Mercy
Prayer, Answers To
Psalm 23
Refuge/Safety
Sorrow
Strength
Suffering
Tired
Weakness

I am in pain and distress; may your salvation, O God, protect me.
(Psalm 69:29)

Be merciful to me, LORD, for I am faint; O LORD, heal me, for my bones are in agony.
(Psalm 6:2)

Heal me, O LORD, and I will be healed; save me and I will be saved, for you are the one I praise.
(Jeremiah 17:14)

O LORD my God, I called to you for help and you healed me.
(Psalm 30:2)

My soul will boast in the LORD; let the afflicted hear and rejoice.
(Psalm 34:2)

For he will deliver the needy who cry out, the afflicted who have no one to help.
(Psalm 72:12)

The LORD will sustain him on his sickbed and restore him from his bed of illness.
(Psalm 41:3)

Everything is possible for him who believes.
(Mark 9:23)

When the sun was setting, the people brought to Jesus all who had various kinds of sickness, and laying his hands on each one, he healed them.
(Luke 4:40)

Don't be afraid; just believe, and she will be healed.
(Luke 8:50)

And the people all tried to touch him, because power
was coming from him and healing them all.
(Luke 6:19)

Jesus had compassion on them and touched their eyes.
Immediately they received their sight and followed him.
(Matthew 20:34)

The blind and the lame came to him at the temple, and he
healed them.
(Matthew 21:14)

Is any of you sick? He should call the elders of the church
to pray over him and anoint him with oil in the name of
the Lord.
(James 5:14)

And the prayer offered in faith will make the sick person
well; the Lord will raise him up.
(James 5:15)

SIN, CONSEQUENCES OF

See also:
Devil
Evil,
Resisting
Forgiveness
Temptation
Unbelief

There will be trouble and distress for every human being who does evil.
(Romans 2:9)

"There is no peace," says my God, "for the wicked."
(Isaiah 57:21)

He who digs a hole and scoops it out falls into the pit he has made. The trouble he causes recoils on himself; his violence comes down on his own head.
(Psalm 7:15-16)

The evil deeds of a wicked man ensnare him; the cords of his sin hold him fast.
(Proverbs 5:22)

The righteousness of the upright delivers them, but the unfaithful are trapped by evil desires.
(Proverbs 11:6)

The sins of some men are obvious, reaching the place of judgment ahead of them; the sins of others trail behind them.
(1 Timothy 5:24)

One sinner destroys much good.
(Ecclesiastes 9:18)

There is something else meaningless that occurs on earth: righteous men who get what the wicked deserve, and wicked men who get what the righteous deserve.
(Ecclesiastes 8:14)

Although a wicked man commits a hundred crimes and still lives a long time, I know that it will go better with God-fearing men, who are reverent before God.
(Ecclesiastes 8:12)

See how the evildoers lie fallen — thrown down, not able to rise!
(Psalm 36:12)

The LORD laughs at the wicked, for he knows their day is coming.
(Psalm 37:13)

For the LORD watches over the way of the righteous, but the way of the wicked will perish.
(Psalm 1:6)

Do not be deceived: God cannot be mocked. A man reaps what he sows.
(Galatians 6:7)

The one who sows to please his sinful nature, from that nature will reap destruction; the one who sows to please the Spirit, from the Spirit will reap eternal life.
(Galatians 6:8)

Everyone who sins breaks the law; in fact, sin is lawlessness.
(1 John 3:4)

God will bring every deed into judgment, including every hidden thing, whether it is good or evil.
(Ecclesiastes 12:14)

If we deliberately keep on sinning after we have received the knowledge of the truth, no sacrifice for sins is left, but only a fearful expectation of judgment and of raging fire that will consume the enemies of God.
(Hebrews 10:26-27)

But because of your stubbornness and you unrepentant heart, you are storing up wrath against yourself for the day of God's wrath, when his righteous judgment will be revealed.
(Romans 2:5)

The evil man has no future hope, and the lamp of the wicked will be snuffed out.
(Proverbs 24:20)

The wrath of God is being revealed from heaven against all the godlessness and wickedness of men.
(Romans 1:18)

On the wicked he will rain fiery coals and burning sulfur; a scorching wind will be their lot.
(Psalm 11:6)

Your own conduct and actions have brought this upon you. This is your punishment. How bitter it is! How it pierces to the heart!
(Jeremiah 4:18)

For I, the LORD your God, am a jealous God, punishing the children for the sin of the fathers to the third and fourth generation of those who hate me, but showing love to a thousand generations of those who love me and keep my commandments.
(Exodus 20:5-6)

If your right eye causes to sin, gouge it out and throw it away. It is better for you to lose one part of your body than for your whole body to be thrown into hell.
(Matthew 5:29)

For the wages of sin is death, but the gift of God is eternal life in Christ Jesus our LORD.
(Romans 6:23)

SINFUL NATURE

See also:
Christ, Mission Of
Christ, Sacrifice Of
Forgive
Forgiveness
Guilt/Shame
Sin, Consequences Of

If we claim to be without sin, we deceive ourselves and the truth is not in us.
(1 John 1:8)

If we claim we have not sinned, we make him out to be a liar and his word has no place in our lives.
(1 John 1:10)

Even from birth the wicked go astray; from the womb they are wayward and speak lies.
(Psalm 58:3)

Man is born to trouble as surely as sparks fly upward.
(Job 5:7)

Your first father sinned; your spokesmen rebelled against me.
(Isaiah 43:27)

Surely I was sinful at birth, sinful from the time my mother conceived me.
(Psalm 51:5)

Therefore, just as sin entered the world through one man, and death through sin, and in this way death came to all men, because all sinned — for before the law was given, sin was in the world.
(Romans 5:12-13)

Here is a trustworthy saying that deserves full acceptance: Christ Jesus came into the world to save sinners — of whom I am the worst.
(1 Timothy 1:15)

There is not a righteous man on earth who does what is right and never sins.
(Ecclesiastes 7:20)

All have turned aside, they have together become corrupt; there is no one who does good, not even one.
(Psalm 14:3)

No one is good — except God alone.
(Mark 10:18)

But I will pass judgment on you because you say, "I have not sinned."
(Jeremiah 2:35)

Who can say, "I have kept my heart pure; I am clean and without sin"?
(Proverbs 20:9)

If any one of you is without sin, let him be the first to throw a stone at her.
(John 8:7)

For whoever keeps the whole law yet stumbles at just one point is guilty of breaking all of it.
(James 2:10)

Anyone, then, who knows the good he ought to do and doesn't do it, sins.
(James 4:17)

But sin is not taken into account when there is no law.
(Romans 5:13)

If I had not come and spoken to them, they would not be guilty of sin. Now, however, they have no excuse for their sin.
(John 15:22)

If you were blind, you would not be guilty of sin; but now that you claim you can see, your guilt remains.
(John 9:41)

I know that nothing good lives in me, that is, in my sinful nature.
(Romans 7:18)

For all have sinned and fall short of the glory of God, and are justified freely by his grace through the redemption that came by Christ Jesus.
(Romans 3:23-24)

So I find this law at work: When I want to do good, evil is right there with me.
(Romans 7:21)

Now if I do what I do not want to do, it is no longer I who do it, but it is sin living in me that does it.
(Romans 7:20)

Keep your servant also from willful sins; may they not rule over me. Then I will be blameless, innocent of great transgression.
(Psalm 19:13)

Not that I have already obtained all this, or have already been made perfect, but I press on to take hold of that for which Christ Jesus took hold of me.
(Philippians 3:12)

SING PRAISES

See also:
Blessings
Joy
Praise Him
Thankful
Worship

I will sing and make music to the LORD.
(Psalm 27:6)

I will sing to the LORD, for he has been good to me.
(Psalm 13:6)

I will praise God's name in song and glorify him with
thanksgiving.
(Psalm 69:30)

For God is the King of all the earth; sing to him a psalm
of praise.
(Psalm 47:7)

Sing joyfully to the LORD, you righteous; it is fitting for
the upright to praise him.
(Psalm 33:1)

Sing to God, O kingdoms of the earth, sing praise to the
Lord.
(Psalm 68:32)

Shout with joy to God, all the earth! Sing the glory of his
name; make his praise glorious!
(Psalm 66:1-2)

Sing to God, sing praise to his name, extol him who rides on
the clouds — his name is the LORD — and rejoice before him.
(Psalm 68:4)

Sing for joy to God our strength; shout aloud to the God
of Jacob! Begin the music, strike the tambourine, play the
melodious harp and lyre.
(Psalm 81:1-2)

It is good to praise the LORD and make music to your name, O Most High, to proclaim your love in the morning and your faithfulness at night.
(Psalm 92:1-2)

Come, let us sing for joy to the LORD; let us shout aloud to the Rock of our salvation.
(Psalm 95:1)

Sing to the LORD a new song; sing to the LORD, all the earth. Sing to the LORD, praise his name; proclaim his salvation day after day.
(Psalm 96:1-2)

Sing to him, sing praise to him; tell of all his wonderful acts.
(Psalm 105:2)

Sing and make music in your heart to the Lord, always giving thanks to God the Father for everything, in the name of our Lord Jesus Christ.
(Ephesians 5:19-20)

I will sing to the LORD all my life; I will sing praise to my God as long as I live.
(Psalm 104:33)

SLANDER

See also:
Communication
Gossip
Lying
Swearing

Brothers, do not slander one another.
(James 4:11)

Do not go about spreading slander among your people.
(Leviticus 19:16)

You shall not give false testimony against your neighbor.
(Exodus 20:16)

Whoever spreads slander is a fool.
(Proverbs 10:18)

With his mouth the godless destroys his neighbor, but
through knowledge the righteous escape.
(Proverbs 11:9)

Not a word from their mouth can be trusted; their heart
is filled with destruction. Their throat is an open grave;
with their tongue they speak deceit.
(Psalm 5:9)

Their tongue is a deadly arrow; it speaks with deceit.
With his mouth each speaks cordially to his neighbor, but
in his heart he sets a trap for him.
(Jeremiah 9:8)

The poison of vipers is on their lips. Their mouths are full
of cursing and bitterness.
(Romans 3:13-14)

You speak continually against your brother and slander
your own mother's son.
(Psalm 50:20)

A man who lacks judgment derides his neighbor, but a man of understanding holds his tongue.
(Proverbs 11:12)

Whoever slanders his neighbor in secret, him will I put to silence.
(Psalm 101:5)

Whoever would love life and see good days must keep his tongue from evil and his lips from deceitful speech.
(1 Peter 3:10)

For by your words you will be acquitted, and by your words you will be condemned.
(Matthew 12:37)

SLEEP PROBLEMS

See also:
Depression, Symptoms Of
Love, By God
Peace
Protection
Refuge/Safety

I will lie down and sleep in peace, for you alone, O LORD, make me dwell in safety.
(Psalm 4:8)

I lie down and sleep; I wake again, because the LORD sustains me.
(Psalm 3:5)

I will praise the LORD who counsels me; even at night my heart instructs me.
(Psalm 16:7)

By day the LORD directs his love, at night his song is with me — a prayer to the God of my life.
(Psalm 42:8)

The sleep of a laborer is sweet, whether he eats little or much, but the abundance of a rich man permits him no sleep.
(Ecclesiastes 5:12)

In vain you rise early and stay up late, toiling for food to eat — for he grants sleep to those he loves.
(Psalm 127:2)

He who dwells in the shelter of the Most High will rest in the shadow of the Almighty.
(Psalm 91:1)

SORROW

Godly sorrow brings repentance that leads to salvation and leaves no regret, but worldly sorrow brings death.
(2 Corinthians 7:10)

They will enter Zion with singing; everlasting joy will crown their heads. Gladness and joy will overtake them, and sorrow and sighing will flee away.
(Isaiah 35:10)

Surely he took up our infirmities and carried our sorrows ....
(Isaiah 53:4)

Jesus wept.
(John 11:35)

Blessed are you who weep now, for you will laugh.
(Luke 6:21)

My soul is overwhelmed with sorrow to the point of death. Stay here and keep watch with me.
(Matthew 26:38)

A happy heart makes the face cheerful, but heartache crushes the spirit.
(Proverbs 15:13)

A cheerful heart is good medicine, but a crushed spirit drys up the bones.
(Proverbs 17:22)

Why are you downcast, O my soul? Why so disturbed within me? Put your hope in God, for I will yet praise him, my Savior and my God.
(Psalm 43:5)

My soul is weary with sorrow; strengthen me according to your word.
(Psalm 119:28)

STRENGTH

It is God who arms me with strength
and makes my way perfect.
(Psalm 18:32)

The LORD is my strength and my song; he has become my salvation.
(Psalm 118:14)

Be strong in the Lord and in his mighty power.
(Ephesians 6:10)

When I called, you answered me; you made me bold and stouthearted.
(Psalm 138:3)

You armed me with strength for battle.
(Psalm 18:39)

He lifted me out of the slimy pit, out of the mud and the mire; he
set my feet on a rock and gave me a firm place to stand.
(Psalm 40:2)

With your help I can advance against a troop; with my
God I can scale a wall.
(Psalm 18:29)

He will keep you strong to the end, so that you will be
blameless on the day of our Lord Jesus Christ.
(1 Corinthians 1:8)

May he strengthen your hearts so that you will be blameless and holy in the presence of our God and Father
when our Lord Jesus comes with all his holy ones.
(1 Thessalonians 3:13)

I love you, O LORD, my strength.
(Psalm 18:1)

SUFFERING

See also:
Death/Dying
Grief
Hardship
Help
Mercy
Prayer, Answers To
Protection
Psalm 23
Refuge/Safety
Sickness
Sorrow
Tired
Troubles

I have suffered much.
(Psalm 119:107)

I have become like broken pottery.
(Psalm 31:12)

Look upon my affliction and my
distress and take away all my sins.
(Psalm 25:18)

Preserve my life, O LORD, according to your word.
(Psalm 119:107)

Look upon my suffering and deliver me, for I have not
forgotten your law.
(Psalm 119:153)

You hear, O LORD, the desire of the afflicted; you encourage them, and you listen to their cry.
(Psalm 10:17)

In my anguish I cried to the LORD, and he answered by
setting me free.
(Psalm 118:5)

I will be glad and rejoice in your love, for you saw my
affliction and knew the anguish of my soul.
(Psalm 31:7)

For he has not despised or disdained the suffering of the
afflicted one; he has not hidden his face from him but has
listened to his cry for help.
(Psalm 22:24)

My comfort in my suffering is this: Your promise preserves my life.
(Psalm 119:50)

For just as the sufferings of Christ flow over into our
lives, so also through Christ our comfort overflows.
(2 Corinthians 1:5)

He was despised and rejected by men, a man of sorrows,
and familiar with suffering.
(Isaiah 53:3)

Therefore, since Christ suffered in his body, arm yourselves also with the same attitude, because he who has
suffered in his body is done with sin.
(1 Peter 4:1)

As a result, he does not live the rest of his earthly life for
evil human desires, but rather for the will of God.
(1 Peter 4:2)

Make us glad for as many days as you have afflicted us,
for as many years as we have seen trouble.
(Psalm 90:15)

Surely it was for my benefit that I suffered such anguish.
(Isaiah 38:17)

It was good for me to be afflicted so that I might learn
your decrees.
(Psalm 119:71)

I have tested you in the furnace of affliction.
(Isaiah 48:10)

We also rejoice in our sufferings, because we know that
suffering produces perseverance; perseverance,
character; and character, hope.
(Romans 5:3-4)

I consider that our present sufferings are not worth
comparing with the glory that will be revealed in us.
(Romans 8:18)

And the God of all grace, who called you to his eternal
glory in Christ, after you have suffered a little while, will
himself restore you and make you strong, firm and
steadfast.
(1 Peter 5:10)

To him be the power for ever and ever. Amen.
(1 Peter 5:11)

SWEARING

See also:
Communication
Gossip
Lying
Slander

You shall not misuse the name of
the LORD your God, for the LORD
will not hold anyone guiltless who
misuses his name.
(Exodus 20:7)

But now you must rid yourselves of all such things as
these: anger, rage, malice, slander, and filthy language
from your lips.
(Colossians 3:8)

Better a poor man whose walk is blameless than a fool
whose lips are perverse.
(Proverbs 19:1)

Do not let your mouth lead you into sin.
(Ecclesiastes 5:6)

Do not let any unwholesome talk come out of your
mouths, but only what is helpful for building others up
according to their needs, that it may benefit those who
listen.
(Ephesians 4:29)

Nor should there be obscenity, foolish talk or coarse
joking, which are out of place, but rather thanksgiving.
(Ephesians 5:4)

If anyone considers himself religious and yet does not
keep a tight rein on his tongue, he deceives himself and
his religion is worthless.
(James 1:26)

Put away perversity from your mouth; keep corrupt talk far from your lips.
(Proverbs 4:24)

The lips of the righteous know what is fitting, but the mouth of the wicked only what is perverse.
(Proverbs 10:32)

Like a fluttering sparrow or a darting swallow, an undeserved curse does not come to rest.
(Proverbs 26:2)

TEMPTATION

See also:
Complacent
Devil
Evil, Resisting
Lord's Prayer

And lead us not into temptation.
(Luke 11:4)

If you think you are standing firm, be careful that you don't fall!
(1 Corinthians 10:12)

No temptation has seized you except what is common to man.
(1 Corinthians 10:13)

And God is faithful; he will not let you be tempted beyond what you can bear.
(1 Corinthians 10:13)

But when you are tempted, he will also provide a way out so that you can stand up under it.
(1 Corinthians 10:13)

When tempted, no one should say, "God is tempting me." For God cannot be tempted by evil, nor does he tempt anyone; but each one is tempted when, by his own evil desire, he is dragged away and enticed.
(James 1:13-14)

Then, after desire has conceived, it gives birth to sin; and sin, when it is full-grown, gives birth to death.
(James 1:15)

Watch and pray so that you will not fall into temptation. The spirit is willing, but the body is weak.
(Matthew 26:41)

Like a muddied spring or a polluted well is a righteous man who gives way to the wicked.
(Proverbs 25:26)

TEN COMMANDMENTS

See also:
Commandments
Disobedience
Obedience
Scripture/Word

1. You shall have no other gods before me.
(Exodus 20:3)

2. You shall not make for yourself an idol in the form of anything in heaven above or on the earth beneath or in the waters below.
(Exodus 20:4)

3. You shall not misuse the name of the LORD your God, for the LORD will not hold anyone guiltless who misuses his name.
(Exodus 20:7)

4. Remember the Sabbath day by keeping it holy.
(Exodus 20:8)

5. Honor your father and your mother, so that you may live long in the land the LORD your God is giving you.
(Exodus 20:12)

6. You shall not murder.
(Exodus 20:13)

7. You shall not commit adultery.
(Exodus 20:14)

8. You shall not steal.
(Exodus 20:15)

9. You shall not give false testimony against your neighbor.
(Exodus 20:16)

10. You shall not covet your neighbor's house. You shall not covet your neighbor's wife, or his manservant or maidservant, his ox or donkey, or anything that belongs to your neighbor.
(Exodus 20:17)

THANKFUL

See also:
Blessings
Joy
Praise Him
Sing Praises
Worship

Give thanks to the LORD Almighty, for the LORD is good; his love endures forever.
(Jeremiah 33:11)

Thanks be to God for his indescribable gift!
(2 Corinthians 9:15)

Let us come before him with thanksgiving and extol him with music and song.
(Psalm 95:2)

Enter his gates with thanksgiving and his courts with praise; give thanks to him and praise his name.
(Psalm 100:4)

I will give you thanks in the great assembly; among throngs of people I will praise you.
(Psalm 35:18)

We give thanks to you, O God, we give thanks, for your Name is near; men tell of your wonderful deeds.
(Psalm 75:1)

Give thanks to the LORD, call on his name; make known among the nations what he has done, and proclaim that his name is exalted.
(Isaiah 12:4)

O LORD my God, I will give you thanks forever.
(Psalm 30:12)

And whatever you do, whether in word or deed, do it all in the name of the Lord Jesus, giving thanks to God the Father through Him.
(Colossians 3:17)

Give thanks to the LORD, for he is good. His love endures forever.
(Psalm 136:1)

THERAPY

See also:
Rebuke/Correction
Scripture/Word
Thinking, Healthy
Thinking, Unhealthy

The purposes of a man's heart are deep waters, but a man of understanding draws them out.
(Proverbs 20:5)

Carry each others's burdens, and in this way you will fulfill the law of Christ.
(Galatians 6:2)

Your statutes are my delight; they are my counselors.
(Psalm 119:24)

Blessed is he who has regard for the weak; the LORD delivers him in times of trouble.
(Psalm 41:1)

We who are strong ought to bear with the failings of the weak and not to please ourselves. Each of us should please his neighbor for his good, to build him up.
(Romans 15:1-2)

THINKING, HEALTHY

See also:
Christ, Personality Of
God, All Knowing
God, First/Only
God, Present Everywhere
Mortal Man
Scripture/Word
Therapy
Thinking, Unhealthy

When I was a child, I talked like a child, I thought like a child, I reasoned like a child. When I became a man, I put childish ways behind me.
(1 Corinthians 13:11)

Brothers, stop thinking like children. In regard to evil be infants, but in your thinking be adults.
(1 Corinthians 14:20)

Forgetting what is behind and straining toward what is ahead, I press on toward the goal to win the prize for which God has called me heavenward in Christ Jesus.
(Philippians 3:13-14)

As water reflects a face, so a man's heart reflects the man.
(Proverbs 27:19)

But we have the mind of Christ.
(1 Corinthians 2:16)

Therefore, holy brothers, who share in the heavenly calling, fix your thoughts on Jesus.
(Hebrews 3:1)

Watch your life and doctrine closely.
(1 Timothy 4:16)

All Scripture is God-breathed and is useful for teaching, rebuking, correcting and training in righteousness, so that the man of God may be thoroughly equipped for every good work.
(2 Timothy 3:16-17)

For the word of God is living and active. Sharper than any double-edged sword, it penetrates even to dividing soul and spirit, joints and marrow; it judges the thoughts and attitudes of the heart.
(Hebrews 4:12)

So I strive always to keep my conscience clear before God and man.
(Acts 24:16)

We demolish arguments and every pretension that sets itself up against the knowledge of God, and we take captive every thought to make it obedient to Christ.
(2 Corinthians 10:5)

Surely you desire truth in the inner parts; you teach me wisdom in the inmost place.
(Psalm 51:6)

Therefore we do not lose heart. Though outwardly we are wasting away, yet inwardly we are being renewed day be day.
(2 Corinthians 4:16)

And this is my prayer: that your love may abound more and more in knowledge and depth of insight, so that you may be able to discern what is best and may be pure and blameless until the day of Christ.
(Philippians 1:9-10)

Create in me a pure heart, O God, and renew a steadfast spirit in me.
(Psalm 51:10)

Those who live in accordance with the Spirit have their minds set on what the Spirit desires.
(Romans 8:5)

You will keep in perfect peace him whose mind is steadfast, because he trusts in you.
(Isaiah 26:3)

Test me, O LORD, and try me, examine my heart and my mind; for your love is ever before me, and I walk continually in your truth.
(Psalm 26:2-3)

Yet you know me, O LORD; you see me and test my thoughts about you.
(Jeremiah 12:3)

The good man brings good things out of the good stored up in his heart, and the evil man brings evil things out of the evil stored up in his heart. For out of the overflow of his heart his mouth speaks.
(Luke 6:45)

He who seeks good finds goodwill, but evil comes to him who searches for it.
(Proverbs 11:27)

The cheerful heart has a continual feast.
(Proverbs 15:15)

Above all else, guard your heart, for it is the wellspring of life.
(Proverbs 4:23)

The man who fears God will avoid all extremes.
(Ecclesiastes 7:18)

Finally, brothers, whatever is true, whatever is noble, whatever is right, whatever is pure, whatever is lovely, whatever is admirable — if anything is excellent or praiseworthy, think about such things.
(Philippians 4:8)

May the words of my mouth and the meditation of my heart be pleasing in your sight, O LORD, my Rock and my Redeemer.
(Psalm 19:14)

Be at rest once more, O my soul, for the LORD has been good to you.
(Psalm 116:7)

THINKING, UNHEALTHY

The LORD detests the thoughts of the wicked, but those of the pure are pleasing to him.
(Proverbs 15:26)

Many live as enemies of the cross of Christ. Their destiny is destruction, their god is their stomach, and their glory is their shame. Their mind is on earthly things.
(Philippians 3:18-19)

Those who live according to the sinful nature have their minds set on what that nature desires.
(Romans 8:5)

How long, O men, will you turn my glory into shame? How long will you love delusions and seek false gods?
(Psalm 4:2)

For although they knew God, they neither glorified him as God nor gave thanks to him, but their thinking became futile and their foolish hearts were darkened.
(Romans 1:21)

In his pride the wicked does not seek him; in all his thoughts there is no room for God.
(Psalm 10:4)

The sinful mind is hostile to God. It does not submit to God's law, nor can it do so.
(Romans 8:7)

The mind of sinful man is death, but the mind controlled by the Spirit is life and peace.
(Romans 8:6)

Let the wicked forsake his way and the evil man his thoughts.
(Isaiah 55:7)

Wash the evil from your heart and be saved. How long will you harbor wicked thoughts?
(Jeremiah 4:14)

For out of the heart come evil thoughts, murder, adultery, sexual immorality, theft, false testimony, slander. These are what make a man "unclean"; but eating with unwashed hands does not make him "unclean."
(Matthew 15:19-20)

How long must I wrestle with my thoughts and every day have sorrow in my heart?...But I trust in your unfailing love; my heart rejoices in your salvation.
(Psalm 13:2-6)

Do not conform any longer to the pattern of this world, but be transformed by the renewing of your mind. Then you will be able to test and approve what God's will is — his good, pleasing and perfect will.
(Romans 12:2)

How much more, then, will the blood of Christ, who through the eternal Spirit offered himself unblemished to God, cleanse our consciences from acts that lead to death, so that we may serve the living God!
(Hebrews 9:14)

TIRED

See also:
Hardship
Help
Hopeless
Mercy
Protection
Refuge/Safety
Sickness
Strength
Suffering
Weakness

*Come to me, all you who are weary
and burdened, and I will give you rest.*
(Matthew 11:28)

For my yoke is easy and my burden is light.
(Matthew 11:30)

My soul finds rest in God alone; my salvation comes from him.
(Psalm 62:1)

He gives strength to the weary, and increases the power of
the weak.
(Isaiah 40:29)

Never tire of doing what is right.
(2 Thessalonians 3:13)

Let us not become weary in doing good, for at the proper
time we will reap a harvest if we do not give up.
(Galatians 6:9)

Never be lacking in zeal, but keep your spiritual fervor,
serving the LORD.
(Romans 12:11)

Consider him who endured such opposition from sinful
men, so that you will not grow weary and lose heart.
(Hebrews 12:3)

To this end I labor, struggling with all his energy, which so
powerfully works in me.
(Colossians 1:29)

Refresh my heart in Christ.
(Philemon 1:20)

TROUBLES

See also:
Disaster
Guidance
Hardship
Help
Mercy
Prayer, Answers To
Protection
Refuge/Safety
Sickness
Strength
Suffering
Tired
Trust
Weakness

Is any one of you in trouble?
He should pray.
(James 5:13)

I pour out my complaint before him; before him I tell my
trouble.
(Psalm 142:2)

*Do not let your hearts be troubled
and do not be afraid.*
(John 14:27)

*In this world you will have trouble. But take heart! I have
overcome the world.*
(John 16:33)

For our light and momentary troubles are achieving for
us an eternal glory that far outweighs them all.
(2 Corinthians 4:17)

Do not be far from me, for trouble is near and there is no
one to help.
(Psalm 22:11)

If you falter in times of trouble, how small is your
strength!
(Proverbs 24:10)

May all who gloat over my distress be put to shame and
confusion.
(Psalm 35:26)

For troubles without number surround me; my sins have overtaken me, and I cannot see. They are more than the hairs of my head, and my heart fails within me.
(Psalm 40:12)

The troubles of my heart have multiplied; free me from my anguish.
(Psalm 25:17)

Though you have made me see troubles, many and bitter, you will restore my life again; from the depths of the earth you will again bring me up.
(Psalm 71:20)

Trouble and distress have come upon me, but your commands are my delight.
(Psalm 119:143)

God is our refuge and strength, an ever-present help in trouble.
(Psalm 46:1)

The LORD is a refuge for the oppressed, a stronghold in times of trouble.
(Psalm 9:9)

The salvation of the righteous comes from the LORD; he is their stronghold in time of trouble.
(Psalm 37:39)

A righteous man may have many troubles, but the LORD delivers him from them all.
(Psalm 34:19)

For in the day of trouble he will keep me safe in his dwelling; he will hide me in the shelter of his tabernacle and set me high upon a rock.
(Psalm 27:5)

He makes me lie down in green pastures, he leads me beside quiet waters, he restores my soul.
(Psalm 23:2-3)

But I will sing of your strength, in the morning I will sing of your love; for you are my fortress, my refuge in times of trouble.
(Psalm 59:16)

Shout for joy, O heavens; rejoice, O earth; burst into song, O mountains! For the LORD comforts his people and will have compassion on his afflicted ones.
(Isaiah 49:13)

Praise be to the God and Father of our Lord Jesus Christ, the Father of compassion and the God of all comfort.
(2 Corinthians 1:3)

Who comforts us in all our troubles, so that we can comfort those in any trouble with the comfort we ourselves have received from God.
(2 Corinthians 1:4)

TRUST

Trust in the LORD with all your heart
and lean not on your own understanding; in all your ways acknowledge him
and, he will make your paths straight.
(Proverbs 3:5-6)

Do not let your hearts be troubled. Trust in God; trust also in me.
(John 14:1)

Let him who walks in the dark, who has no light, trust in
the name of the LORD and rely on his God.
(Isaiah 50:10)

Many are the woes of the wicked, but the LORD'S unfailing love surrounds the man who trusts in him.
(Psalm 32:10)

You are my God; save your servant who trusts in you.
(Psalm 86:2)

Some trust in chariots and some in horses, but we trust in
the name of the LORD our God.
(Psalm 20:7)

But as for me, I trust in you.
(Psalm 55:23)

Trust in the LORD forever, for the LORD, the LORD, is the
Rock eternal.
(Isaiah 26:4)

Blessed is the man who trusts in the LORD, whose confidence is in him.
(Jeremiah 17:7)

Trust in him at all times, O people; pour out your hearts to him, for God is our refuge.
(Psalm 62:8)

Blessed is the man who makes the LORD his trust.
(Psalm 40:4)

Those who know your name will trust in you, for you, LORD, have never forsaken those who seek you.
(Psalm 9:10)

Anyone who trusts in him will never be put to shame.
(Romans 10:11)

Those who trust in the LORD are like Mount Zion, which cannot be shaken but endures forever.
(Psalm 125:1)

For the king trusts in the LORD; through the unfailing love of the Most High he will not be shaken.
(Psalm 21:7)

To you, O LORD, I lift up my soul; in you I trust, O my God.
(Psalm 25:1)

In him our hearts rejoice, for we trust in his holy name.
(Psalm 33:21)

Trust in the LORD and do good.
(Psalm 37:3)

Let the morning bring me word of your unfailing love, for I have put my trust in you.
(Psalm 143:8)

I am like an olive tree flourishing in the house of God; I trust in God's unfailing love for ever and ever.
(Psalm 52:8)

TRUTH

See also:
Confusion
Commandments
Dissatisfaction
Evil, Resisting
Light
Lying
Obedience
Scripture/Word
Wisdom

God our Savior…wants all men to be saved
and to come to a knowledge of the truth.
(1 Timothy 2:3-4)

He chose to give us birth through the
word of truth, that we might be a
kind of first-fruits of all he created.
(James 1:18)

O Lord, do not your eyes look for truth?
(Jeremiah 5:3)

Surely you desire truth in the inner parts; you teach me
wisdom in the inmost place.
(Psalm 51:6)

Teach me your way, O LORD, and I will walk in your truth.
(Psalm 86:11)

Test me, O LORD, and try me, examine my heart and my
mind; for your love is ever before me, and I walk continually in your truth.
(Psalm 26:2-3)

Send forth your light and your truth, let them guide me; let them
bring me to your holy mountain, to the place where you dwell.
(Psalm 43:3)

We have seen his glory, the glory of the One and Only,
who came from the Father, full of grace and truth.
(John 1:14)

*I am the way and the truth and the life. No one comes to the
Father except through me.*
(John 14:6)

If you hold to my teaching, you are really my disciples. Then you will know the truth, and the truth will set you free.
(John 8:31-32)

But whoever lives by the truth comes into the light, so that it may be seen plainly that what he has done through God.
(John 3:21)

When the Counselor comes, whom I will send to you from the Father, the Spirit of truth who goes out from the Father, he will testify about me.
(John 15:26)

But when he, the Spirit of truth, comes, he will guide you into all truth.
(John 16:13)

May your love and your truth always protect me.
(Psalm 40:11)

The Lord is near to all who call on him, to all who call on him in truth.
(Psalm 145:18)

Buy the truth and do not sell it; get wisdom, discipline and understanding.
(Proverbs 23:23)

I have chosen the way of truth; I have set my heart on your laws.
(Psalm 119:30)

Stand firm then, with the belt of truth buckled around your waist, with the breastplate of righteousness in place, and with your feet fitted with the readiness that comes from the gospel of peace.
(Ephesians 6:14-15)

But for those who are self-seeking and who reject the truth and follow evil, there will be wrath and anger.
(Romans 2:8)

Those who oppose him he must gently instruct, in the hope that God will grant them repentance leading them to a knowledge of the truth, and that they will come to their senses and escape from the trap of the devil, who has taken them captive to do his will.
(2 Timothy 2:25-26)

He was a murderer from the beginning, not holding to the truth, for there is no truth in him.
(John 8:44)

They perish because they refused to love the truth and so be saved. For this reason, God sends them a powerfuil delusion so that they will believe the lie and so that all will be condemned who have not believed the truth but have delighted in wickedness.
(2 Thessalonians 2:10-12)

Dear children, let us not love with words or tongue but with actions and in truth.
(1 John 3:18)

But we ought always to thank God for you, brothers loved by the Lord, because from the beginning God chose you to be saved through the sanctifying work of the Spirit and through belief in the truth.
(2 Thessalonians 2:13)

Now that you have purified yourselves by obeying the truth so that you have sincere love for your brothers, love one another deeply, from the heart.
(1 Peter 1:22)

UNBELIEF

See also:
Backsliding
Belief
Complacent
Darkness
Denial
Doubt
Hell
Repent

The fool says in his heart, "There is no God."
(Psalm 14:1)

Those who turn away from you will be written in the dust because they have forsaken the LORD, the spring of living water.
(Jeremiah 17:13)

Whoever does not believe stands condemned already because he has not believed in the name of God's one and only Son.
(John 3:18)

Whoever believes in the Son has eternal life, but whoever rejects the Son will not see life, for God's wrath remains on him.
(John 3:36)

The words I have spoken to you are spirit and they are life. Yet there are some of you who do not believe.
(John 6:63)

You diligently study the Scriptures because you think that by them you possess eternal life. These are the Scriptures that testify about me, yet you refuse to come to me to have life.
(John 5:39-40)

Unless you people see miraculous signs and wonders, Jesus told him, *you will never believe.*
(John 4:48)

Even after Jesus had done all these miraculous signs in their presence, they still would not believe in him.
(John 12:37)

For even his own brothers did not believe in him.
(John 7:5)

If they do not listen to Moses and the Prophets, they will not be convinced even if someone rises from the dead.
(Luke 16:31)

I told you that you would die in your sins; if you do not believe that I am the one I claim to be, you will indeed die in your sins.
(John 8:24)

If you are the Christ," they said, "tell us." Jesus answered, *If I tell you, you will not believe me, and if I asked you, you would not answer.*
(Luke 22:67-68)

Can any of you prove me guilty of sin? If I am telling the truth, why don't you believe me?
(John 8:46)

O unbelieving generation, Jesus replied, *how long shall I stay with you? How long shall I put up with you?*
(Mark 9:19)

The fool says in his heart, "There is no God."
(Psalm 53:1)

VENGEANCE

See also:
Anger
Forgive
Hatred
Judgmental
Love, For Others
Peace

Do not seek revenge or bear a grudge against one of your people, but love your neighbor as yourself. I am the LORD.
(Leviticus 19:18)

Make sure that nobody pays back wrong for wrong, but always try to be kind to each other and to everyone else.
(1 Thessalonians 5:15)

Love your enemies, do good to those who hate you.
(Luke 6:27)

You have heard that it was said, "Eye for eye, and tooth for tooth." But I tell you, Do not resist an evil person. If someone strikes you on the right cheek, turn to him the other also.
(Matthew 5:38-39)

If someone takes your cloak, do not stop him from taking your tunic.
(Luke 6:29)

Give to everyone who asks you, and if anyone takes what belongs to you, do not demand it back.
(Luke 6:30)

Do to others as you would have them do to you.
(Luke 6:31)

Love your enemies, do good to them, and lend to them without expecting to get anything back. Then your reward will be great, and you will be sons of the Most High, because he is kind to the ungrateful and wicked.
(Luke 6:35)

If your brother sins against you, go and show him his fault, just between the two of you. If he listens to you, you have won your brother over.
(Matthew 18:15)

But if he will not listen, take one or two others along, so that "every matter may be established by the testimony of two or three witnesses."
(Matthew 18:16)

If he refuses to listen to them, tell it to the church; and if he refuses to listen to the church, treat him as you would a pagan or a tax collector.
(Matthew 18:17)

Do not say, "I'll pay you back for this wrong!" Wait for the LORD, and he will deliver you.
(Proverbs 20:22)

Do not take revenge, my friends, but leave room for God's wrath, for it is written: "It is mine to avenge; I will repay," says the Lord.
(Romans 12:19)

Do not gloat when your enemy falls; when he stumbles, do not let your heart rejoice.
(Proverbs 24:17)

If your enemy is hungry, give him food to eat; if he is thirsty, give him water to drink. In doing this, you will heap burning coals on his head and the LORD will reward you.
(Proverbs 25:21-22)

Do not repay evil with evil or insult with insult, but with blessing, because to this you were called so that you may inherit a blessing.
(1 Peter 3:9)

And one of them struck the servant of the high priest, cutting off his right ear. But Jesus answered, *No more of this.* And he touched the man's ear and healed him.
(Luke 22:50-51)

Put your sword back in its place, Jesus said to him, *for all who draw the sword will die by the sword.*
(Matthew 26:52)

When they hurled their insults at him, he did not retaliate; when he suffered, he made no threats. Instead, he entrusted himself to him who judges justly.
(1 Peter 2:23)

Father, forgive them, for they do not know what they are doing.
(Luke 23:34)

WEAKNESS

See also:
God, All Powerful
Help
Hopeless
Prayer, Answers To
Protection
Refuge/Safety
Strength
Tired
Trust

Look to the LORD and his strength;
seek his face always.
(Psalm 105:4)

The LORD upholds all those who
fall and lifts up all who are bowed
down.
(Psalm 145:14)

He reached down from on high and took hold of me; he
drew me out of deep waters.
(Psalm 18:16)

You give me your shield of victory, and your right hand
sustains me; you stoop down to make me great.
(Psalm 18:35)

He rescued me from my powerful enemy, from my foes,
who were too strong for me.
(Psalm 18:17)

Be strong and take heart, all you who hope in the LORD.
(Psalm 31:24)

God chose the weak things of the world to shame the
strong.
(1 Corinthians 1:27)

My grace is sufficient for you, for my power is made
perfect in weakness.
(2 Corinthians 12:9)

Therefore I will boast all the more gladly about my weaknesses, so that Christ's power may rest on me.
(2 Corinthians 12:9)

That is why, for Christ's sake, I delight in weaknesses, in insults, in hardships, in persecutions, in difficulties.
(2 Corinthians 12:10)

For when I am weak, then I am strong.
(2 Corinthians 12:10)

The body that is sown is perishable, it is raised imperishable; it is sown in dishonor, it is raised in glory; it is sown in weakness, it is raised in power; it is sown a natural body, it is raised a spiritual body.
(1 Corinthians 15:42-44)

Even youths grow tired and weary, and young men stumble and fall; but those who hope in the LORD will renew their strength.
(Isaiah 40:30-31)

They will soar on wings like eagles; they will run and not grow weary, they will walk and not be faint.
(Isaiah 40:31)

I can do everything through him who gives me strength.
(Philippians 4:13)

WILL OF GOD

See also:
Blessings
Christ, Mission Of
Discipline
Joy
Lord's Prayer
Occupation/Job/Work
Peace
Plans
Self-Sacrifice
Servant

Your will be done on earth as it is in heaven.
(Matthew 6:10)

Not everyone who says to me, "Lord, Lord," will enter the kingdom of heaven, but only he who does the will of my Father who is in heaven.
(Matthew 7:21)

Therefore do not be foolish, but understand what the Lord's will is.
(Ephesians 5:17)

You need to persevere so that when you have done the will of God, you will receive what he has promised.
(Hebrews 10:36)

The world and its desires pass away, but the man who does the will of God lives forever.
(1 John 2:17)

Submit yourselves, then, to God.
(James 4:7)

We have not stopped praying for you and asking God to fill you with the knowledge of his will through all spiritual wisdom and understanding.
(Colossians 1:9)

Teach me to do your will, for you are my God; may your good Spirit lead me on level ground.
(Psalm 143:10)

I desire to do your will, O my God; your law is within
my heart.
(Psalm 40:8)

If anyone chooses to do God's will, he will find out whether my
teaching comes from God or whether I speak on my own.
(John 7:17)

For I have come down from heaven not to do my will but to do
the will of him who sent me.
(John 6:38)

Who are my mother and my brothers? he asked. Then he
looked at those seated in a circle around him and said,
Here are my mother and my brothers! Whoever does God's will
is my brother and sister and mother.
(Mark 3:33-35)

Father, if you are willing, take this cup from me; yet not my
will, but yours be done.
(Luke 22:42)

Continue to work out your salvation with fear and trem-
bling, for it is God who works in you to will and to act
according to his good purpose.
(Philippians 2:12-13)

And he made known to us the mystery of his will according to his good pleasure, which he purposed in Christ, to
be put into effect when the times will have reached their
fulfillment — to bring all things in heaven and on earth
together under one head, even Christ.
(Ephesians 1:9-10)

May the God of peace...equip you with everything good
for doing his will, and may he work in us what is pleasing to him, through Jesus Christ, to whom be glory for
ever and ever. Amen.
(Hebrews 13:20-21)

WISDOM

The fear of the LORD is the
beginning of wisdom, and
knowledge of the Holy One
is understanding.
(Proverbs 9:10)

We speak of God's secret wisdom, a wisdom that has been
hidden and that God destined
for our glory before time began.
(1 Corinthians 2:7)

How long will you simple ones love your simple ways?
How long will mockers delight in mockery and fools hate
knowledge?
(Proverbs 1:22)

You who are simple, gain prudence; you who are foolish, gain understanding.
(Proverbs 8:5)

Lips that speak knowledge are a rare jewel.
(Proverbs 20:15)

A fool finds no pleasure in understanding but delights in
airing his own opinions.
(Proverbs 18:2)

Wise men store up knowledge, but the mouth of a fool
invites ruin.
(Proverbs 10:14)

The wise inherit honor, but fools he holds up to shame.
(Proverbs 3:35)

Teach me knowledge and good judgment, for I believe in
your commands.
(Psalm 119:66)

Stay away from a foolish man, for you will not find
knowledge on his lips.
(Proverbs 14:7)

A fool's mouth is his undoing, and his lips are a snare to
his soul.
(Proverbs 18:7)

Wisdom is sweet to your soul; if you find it, there is a
future hope for you, and your hope will not be cut off.
(Proverbs 24:14)

The way of the fool seems right to him, but a wise man
listens to advice.
(Proverbs 12:15)

Wisdom will save you from the ways of wicked men,
from men whose words are perverse, who leave the
straight paths to walk in dark ways, who delight in doing
wrong and rejoice in the perverseness of evil, whose
paths are crooked and who are devious in their ways.
(Proverbs 2:12-15)

Blessed is the man who finds wisdom, the man who
gains understanding, for she is more profitable than
silver and yields better returns than gold.
(Proverbs 3:13-14)

Buy the truth and do not sell it; get wisdom, discipline
and understanding.
(Proverbs 23:23)

Wisdom makes one wise man more powerful than ten rulers in a city.
(Ecclesiastes 7:19)

Wisdom is a shelter as money is a shelter, but the advantage of knowledge is this: that wisdom preserves the life of its possessor.
(Ecclesiastes 7:12)

But the wisdom that comes from heaven is first of all pure; then peace-loving, considerate, submissive, full of mercy and good fruit, impartial and sincere.
(James 3:17)

It is the spirit in a man, the breath of the Almighty, that gives him understanding.
(Job 32:8)

For whoever finds me [Wisdom] finds life and receives favor from the LORD. But whoever fails to find me harms himself; all who hate me love death.
(Proverbs 8:35-36)

Whoever is wise, let him heed these things and consider the great love of the LORD.
(Psalm 107:43)

WITNESS

See also:
Christ, Resurrection Of
Fruitful
Gifts, Spiritual
Self-Sacrifice

*Go into all the world and preach
the good news to all creation.*
(Mark 16:15)

As you sent me into the world, I have sent them into the world.
(John 17:18)

We are therefore Christ's ambassadors, as though God
were making his appeal through us.
(2 Corinthians 5:20)

*I am sending you to them to open their eyes and turn them
from darkness to light, and from the power of Satan to God, so
that they may receive forgiveness of sins and a place among
those who are sanctified by faith in me.*
(Acts 26:17-18)

*What I tell you in the dark, speak in the daylight; what is
whispered in your ear, proclaim from the roofs.*
(Matthew 10:27)

*Come, follow me, Jesus said, and I will make you fishers of
men.*
(Mark 1:17)

Then I heard the voice of the Lord saying, "Whom shall I
send? And who will go for us?" And I said, "Here am I.
Send me!"
(Isaiah 6:8)

I will follow you, Lord; but first let me go back and say
good-by to my family. Jesus replied, *No one who puts his hand
to the plow and looks back is fit for service in the kingdom of God.*
(Luke 9:61-62)

How beautiful are the feet of those who bring good news!
(Romans 10:15)

Blessed are those who have learned to acclaim you, who
walk in the light of your presence, O LORD.
(Psalm 89:15)

*No one who has left home or wife or brothers or parents or
children for the sake of the kingdom of God will fail to receive
many times as much in this age and, in the age to come, eternal
life.*
(Luke 18:29-30)

Rescue those being led away to death; hold back those
staggering toward slaughter.
(Proverbs 24:11)

You will receive power when the Holy Spirit comes on
you; and you will be my witnesses...to the ends of the
earth.
(Acts 1:8)

*Therefore go and make disciples of all nations, baptizing them
in the name of the Father and of the Son and of the Holy Spirit,
and teaching them to obey everything I have commanded you.*
(Matthew 28:19-20)

WIVES

See also:
Adultery
Communication
Divorce
Husbands
Marriage
Marriage Guidance
Sex, Normal

The LORD God said, "It is not good for the man to be alone. I will make a helper suitable for him."
(Genesis 2:18)

Your desire will be for your husband, and he will rule over you.
(Genesis 3:16)

Now I want you to realize that the head of every man is Christ, and the head of the woman is man, and the head of Christ is God.
(1 Corinthians 11:3)

Now as the church submits to Christ, so also wives should submit to their husbands in everything.
(Ephesians 5:24)

Wives, submit to your husbands as to the Lord.
(Ephesians 5:22)

Wives, submit to your husbands, as is fitting in the Lord.
(Colossians 3:18)

Your beauty should not come from outward adornment, such as braided hair and the wearing of gold jewelry and fine clothes. Instead, it should be that of your inner self, the unfading beauty of a gentle and quiet spirit, which is of great worth in God's sight.
(1 Peter 3:3-4)

I also want women to dress modestly, with decency and propriety, not with braided hair or gold or pearls or

expensive clothes, but with good deeds, appropriate for
women who profess to worship God.
(1 Timothy 2:9-10)

Wives, in the same way be submissive to your husbands
so that, if any of them do not believe the word, they may
be won over without words by the behavior of their
wives, when they see the purity and reverence of your
lives.
(1 Peter 3:1-2)

A wife of noble character is her husband's crown, but a
disgraceful wife is like decay in his bones.
(Proverbs 12:4)

Houses and wealth are inherited from parents, but a
prudent wife is from the LORD.
(Proverbs 19:14)

In the same way, their wives are to be women worthy of
respect, not malicious talkers but temperate and trustworthy in everything.
(1 Timothy 3:11)

A wife of noble character who can find? She is worth far
more than rubies. Her husband has full confidence in her
and lacks nothing of value.
(Proverbs 31:10-11)

She is clothed with strength and dignity; she can laugh at
the days to come. She speaks with wisdom, and faithful
instruction is on her tongue. She watches over the affairs
of her household and does not eat the bread of idleness.
(Proverbs 31:25-27)

Charm is deceptive, and beauty is fleeting; but a woman
who fears the LORD is to be praised.
(Proverbs 31:30)

WORLDLY

See also:
Envy/Jealousy
Greedy/Stingy
Money
Poverty
Riches, Beware Of
Riches, True
Self-Sacrifice

Do not love the world or anything in the world. If anyone loves the world, the love of the Father is not in him.
(1 John 2:15)

Dear friends, I urge you, as aliens and strangers in the world, to abstain from sinful desires, which war against your soul.
(1 Peter 2:11)

As long as we are at home in the body we are away from the Lord.
(2 Corinthians 5:6)

For everything in the world — the cravings of sinful man, the lust of his eyes and the boasting of what he has and does — comes not from the Father but from the world.
(1 John 2:16)

What good is it for a man to gain the whole world, yet forfeit his soul?
(Mark 8:36)

The world and its desires pass away, but the man who does the will of God lives forever.
(1 John 2:17)

For we brought nothing into the world, and we can take nothing out of it. But if we have food and clothing, we will be content with that.
(1 Timothy 6:7-8)

So from now on we regard no one from a worldly point
of view. Though we once regarded Christ in this way, we
do so no longer.
(2 Corinthians 5:16)

You adulterous people, don't you know that friendship
with the world is hatred toward God? Anyone who
chooses to be a friend of the world becomes an enemy of
God.
(James 4:4)

You have lived on earth in luxury and self-indulgence.
You have fattened yourselves in the day of slaughter.
(James 5:5)

*What is highly valuable among men is detestable in God's
sight.*
(Luke 16:15)

*Do not store up for yourselves treasures on earth, where moth
and rust destroy, and where thieves break in and steal. But
store up for yourselves treasures in heaven, where moth and
rust do not destroy, and where thieves do not break in and
steal. For where your treasure is, there your heart will be also.*
(Matthew 6:19-21)

WORSHIP

See also:
Joy
Praise Him
Sing Praises
Thankful

Worship the Lord your God and serve him only.
(Luke 4:8)

Come, let us bow down in worship, let us kneel before the LORD our Maker; for he is our God and we are the people of his pasture, the flock under his care.
(Psalm 95:6)

Worship the LORD in the splendor of his holiness; tremble before him, all the earth.
(Psalm 96:9)

Exalt the LORD our God and worship at his footstool; he is holy.
(Psalm 99:5)

Worship the LORD with gladness; come before him with joyful songs.
(Psalm 100:2)

Let all God's angels worship him.
(Hebrews 1:6)

All the earth bows down to you; they sing praise to you, they sing praise to your name.
(Psalm 66:4)

Praise the LORD, O my soul, and forget not all his benefits — who forgives all your sins and heals all your diseases, who redeems your life from the pit and crowns you with love and compassion, who satisfies your desires with good things so that your youth is renewed like the eagle's.
(Psalm 103:2-5)

Therefore, I urge you, brothers, in view of God's mercy,
to offer your bodies as living sacrifices, holy and pleasing
to God — this is your spiritual act of worship.
(Romans 12:1)

Yet a time is coming and has now come when the true worship-
ers will worship the Father in spirit and truth, for they are the
kind of worshipers the Father seeks.
(John 4:23)

God is spirit, and his worshipers must worship in spirit
and in truth.
(John 4:24)